D-DAY THROUGH FRENCH EYES

MARY LOUISE
ROBERTS

D-DAY THROUGH
FRENCH EYES

Normandy 1944

The University of Chicago Press
Chicago and London

The University of Chicago Press, Chicago 60637
The University of Chicago Press, Ltd., London
© 2014 by The University of Chicago
All rights reserved. No part of this book may be used or
reproduced in any manner whatsoever without written permission,
except in the case of brief quotations in critical articles and reviews.
For more information, contact the University of Chicago Press,
1427 E. 60th St., Chicago, IL 60637.
Published 2014
Paperback edition 2022
Printed in the United States of America

31 30 29 28 27 26 25 24 23 22   1 2 3 4 5

ISBN-13: 978-0-226-13699-8 (cloth)
ISBN-13: 978-0-226-82107-8 (paper)
ISBN-13: 978-0-226-13704-9 (e-book)
DOI: https://doi.org/10.7208/chicago/9780226137049.001.0001

Library of Congress Cataloging-in-Publication Data

Roberts, Mary Louise, author.
    D-Day through French eyes : Normandy 1944 / Mary
Louise Roberts.
    pages   cm
    Includes bibliographical references and index.
    ISBN 978-0-226-13699-8 (hardcover : alk. paper) —
ISBN 978-0-226-13704-9 (e-book) 1. World War, 1939–
1945—Campaigns—France—Normandy—Personal
narratives, French. I. Title.
    D756.5.N6R595 2014
    940.54'21421092—dc23

                                            2013040601

♾ This paper meets the requirements of ANSI/NISO Z39.48-1992
(Permanence of Paper).

For Sue

CONTENTS

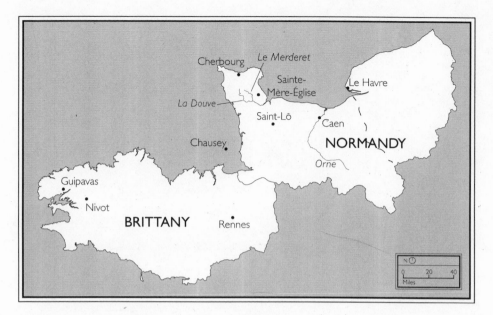

FIGURE 1a. Map of Brittany and Normandy, France.

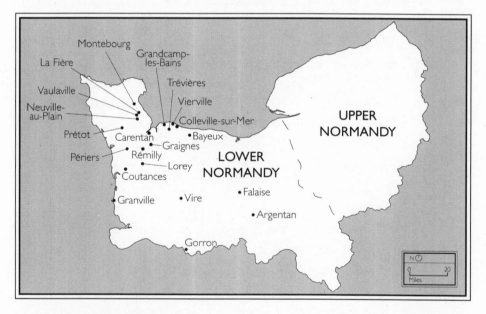

FIGURE 1b. Map of Normandy.

INTRODUCTION

At the mention of D-Day, most Americans summon the image of GIs landing on Omaha Beach in Normandy, France. These first steps onto Nazi-occupied soil, immortalized in a photograph often attributed to Robert Capa, dominate our perceptions of World War II. But did you ever wonder how the landings looked from the opposite direction—to the French onshore? What was D-Day like for the Normans?

US historians have told and retold the story of the Normandy Invasion. But in most accounts, the focus remains on the day-to-day fighting of the Allied forces, particularly the American GIs. As a result, the experience of the Normans has been almost completely ignored. To remedy this, the collection of documents gathered in this book will widen our view by presenting D-Day and the Normandy Campaign through French eyes. Among these documents are *témoignages*, or testimonies, of the campaign culled from French archives and publications.

While acknowledging the British and Canadian contributions to the Normandy Campaign, I have selected testimonies that focus on the American experience of battle. Besides wanting to reach a specifically American audience, I felt the need to limit the project in some way, given the outpouring of memoirs since the fiftieth anniversary of the landings. I have chosen *témoignages* that revolve

FIGURE 2. The GIs land on the shores of Normandy.

around the rich sensory details of D-Day—the sound of artillery, the first glimpse of an American, the stench of death, and the taste of chocolate. The result is a vision of both hell at the hands of the occupiers and joy at being liberated. My purpose is not to give a definitive account of the Normans and their liberators. Rather, I aim to revisit the battle as it was seen by ordinary people. My vantage point is not the London war room but the Norman farmhouse. That perspective, I believe, affords not only a graphic view of the battle but also a very intimate portrait of the American GIs as they fought, suffered, and made friends during the summer of 1944.[1]

The Normandy Invasion, also known as Operation Overlord, has become so famous as to hardly need an introduction. The campaign began on "D-Day," June 6, 1944, in the fifth year of World War II, the most immense and costly war in history. By 1944, the US military had been deployed in two separate theaters. In the Pacific theater of operations, the GIs were fighting the Japanese, who had attacked the United States in December of 1941. In the European theater, the

GIs joined the British and Canadian armies to fight the Germans, whose military aggression had begun in 1939 against Poland. At the peak of Hitler's power in 1942, his forces occupied much of Europe, North Africa, and the Soviet Union.

The German conquest of France in the spring of 1940 led to the creation of a French collaborationist state known as the Vichy regime. The Nazis divided the French nation into two zones, roughly split between north and south. In the southern "free" zone, the Vichy government maintained sovereignty under the leadership of Philippe Pétain. In the northern "occupied" zone, which included the entire western coast, Pétain's collaborationist state retained only limited authority. The German Wehrmacht maintained a strong presence there in anticipation of an Anglo-American invasion along the Atlantic coast. This dual-zone structure collapsed in November 1942, when Allied forces created a new front in northern Africa. At this time, the Germans occupied all of France.

Pétain justified his collaborationist state on the grounds that it would save the French from the worst excesses of German rule. In fact, it did not. Under the guise of "occupation costs," the Nazis drained France of every natural resource as well as food and other basic necessities. Two million Frenchmen were detained as prisoners of war, forced laborers, and deportees. Jews and other "undesirables" were persecuted, then deported east; most did not return. Following the liberation of the country in 1944, the exiled general Charles de Gaulle emerged to claim national sovereignty for the French. Vichy officials fled, were arrested, or were summarily shot by local Resistance forces. Pétain was sentenced to death for treason. For the French people, then, the Liberation was joyful but also chaotic and confusing. Besides the devastating effects of a war fought on their own soil, they had to deal with political uncertainty and the shame of collaboration as well as the humiliation of diminished national prestige.

For the Allies, by contrast, Normandy was a moment of triumph.

The Americans first joined forces with the British and the Canadians against the Germans in North Africa in late 1942. After a terrible struggle in the Tunisian desert, these Allied forces established a foothold there. In July 1943, they moved northward to conquer Sicily, and in September of that year began a long, very difficult campaign for continental Italy. Their efforts in France would succeed rapidly by comparison. Although the Allies met fierce German resistance in Normandy, they were in Paris by the end of August, ten weeks after the invasion began. By contrast, Rome eluded liberation for a full nine months after they first stepped onto southern Italian soil. Although the road from Paris to Berlin was no easy journey, they triumphed over the Germans within a year of the landings. By August 1945, the Americans, along with the British and Canadian forces, were victorious in both the European and the Pacific theaters of war. The United States stood, to use Churchill's phrase, at the "summit of the world."

The war's outcome, then, was glorious for the Americans and humiliating for the French. This difference in fates between the two nations has shaped how US historians have told the story of Normandy. In most American accounts, the French are almost completely left out of the picture, appearing only at the peripheries of the campaign. The contributions of the French army and the organized civilian Resistance are dramatically underplayed. Although General Dwight Eisenhower equated the effectiveness of the Resistance in Normandy with a full fifteen military divisions,[2] French civilians are portrayed nonetheless as inert bystanders at their own liberation.

In fact, Normans were far from passive observers. They participated far more in the battle than has been recognized by US historians. They also suffered more. The first two days of the invasion alone resulted in three thousand deaths, a figure equaling Allied losses during this period.[3] Overall, an estimated 19,890 French civilians lost their lives in the Invasion of Normandy. Both before and after the landings, the entire region was subject to bombardment. In an effort to thwart German advancement by destroying transportation networks and industrial sites throughout northern France, Allied bombers unintentionally destroyed homes and killed civilians. Hundreds of thousands of Normans lost everything they had. Such "collateral damage" was caused by inaccuracy on the part of the bombers. Even in perfect weather, only about half the bombs released at sixteen thousand feet fell within a quarter mile of their target.[4]

Yet despite the hardship, civilians rose to the challenges presented by the war. On the night of June 5–6, they rescued the paratroopers who had slipped into the region by air. They provided Allied infantrymen with intelligence on German artillery strength and troop positions. Entire villages joined forces to hide downed pilots and to care for the wounded. In Brittany, the French Resistance played a major role in fighting the Germans—so much so that General George Patton's Third Army could advance quickly through the region. In countless ways, the Normans were agents in their own liberation.

Looking at D-Day through French eyes, then, reveals the passionate involvement of civilians in the battle. In addition, it affords a close-up view of American GIs during the summer of 1944. The troops spent most of that period on the Cotentin Peninsula in the northwest corner of France (see map). They landed on its eastern shores, then fought west and north to conquer Cherbourg on June 26 and transform its harbor into a supply port. Then the GIs moved southward. Their advance slowed at the base of the Cotentin as they struggled with the challenges of combat in hedgerow country. In late July, Operation Cobra, a combined force of massive bombing and focused attack, enabled the Americans to "break out" of that landscape. Under the direction of General Patton, the newly formed Third Army moved southwest through Brittany. The remaining US forces fought to the south and east, meeting up with the British north of Falaise. After trapping the Germans between Falaise and Argentan, the Americans advanced to the east. By the end of August, they were in Paris.

With clear eyes and honest hearts, Normans witnessed this American journey. Their testimonies in the pages that follow tell their story. Wherever possible, these accounts have been checked against the historical record. But their precision and detail attest to their reliability. Boastful or overly heroic accounts have been excluded on the premise that they are untruthful. Nevertheless, a quiet heroism does emerge in these testimonies. In the summer of 1944, ordinary Normans committed themselves to small but substantial acts of courage. They sought to act like French patriots and, more important, good fathers and mothers, husbands and wives, sisters and brothers, neighbors and friends. In the process, they helped to win their freedom.

CHAPTER ONE

THE NIGHT OF ALL NIGHTS

For Normans, the invasion began with noise. Just before midnight on Monday night, the fifth of June, hundreds of airplanes could be heard flying south over the Cotentin Peninsula. The constant rumble of plane engines and the distant roar of artillery—these two sounds combined to create what one witness called "a ceaseless storm." Together they awakened thousands of Normans from their deepest sleep of the night. They rose from their beds, ran outside in their nightclothes, peered at the sky, and tried to figure out what was happening. *Is this it?* they wondered, overcome with fear and excitement.

The sound of airplanes was by no means a novel phenomenon. In the past months, civilians had grown accustomed to planes flying overhead—hundreds of them—almost every night. Allied bombing of strategic sights throughout northern France had become a common event. But this night was different; something new was happening. The aircraft were flying close to the ground and reaching targets. In response, German machine guns and artillery were firing furiously, contributing to the din. Soon the Norman night was filled with strange sights as well as sounds: the landing of parachutes and gliders, the dancing lights of artillery, the red glow of villages in flames. These sights were terrible, frightening, but also oddly beautiful.

"THEY LAND AS IF IN A DREAM"

In her memoir, Madame Hamel-Hateau, a schoolteacher in Neuville-au-Plain, near Sainte-Mère-Église, captures the dreamlike magic of the night of June 5–6. Hamel-Hateau lived close to the village school and spoke some English. The paratrooper she meets is a pathfinder sent to illuminate the landing areas for thousands of paratroopers who would soon land in Normandy to begin the invasion. He is one of the very first American servicemen to arrive in France.

In the month of June, the days no longer have an end and the night is really just a long twilight because the darkness is never complete. Around 10:00 p.m. this Monday, the fifth of June, I have just gone to bed next to my mother. We are both sleeping on a daybed that we open up every night in the common room. Since the evacuation of Cherbourg, we have given our bedroom to my grandparents. The daybed faces the window, itself wide open on the night. In this way, from my bed, I am taking a moment to reflect on the end of this beautiful day. With sadness I think of a similar June night in 1940 when my boyfriend, Jean, had left to join the Free French. I had received news that he had landed in North Africa, so perhaps he was now in Italy? *Perhaps it will be soon . . .* I thought, but then refused to let my mind wander further. It was time to go to sleep.

Abruptly, the noise of airplanes breaks the night's silence. We have gotten used to that sound. Since there are no military targets here and the railway is more than five miles away, we normally do not pay much attention. But the noise gets louder, and the sky begins to light up and get red. I rise out of bed, and soon the whole family is up as well. We go out into the courtyard. There everything seems calm. The only thing you can hear is the distant murmur of a bombardment in the direction of Quinéville. Yet there seems to be an endless number of planes mysteriously roaming about; their engines create an incessant hum. Then the noise decreases and becomes vague and distant. "It's just like the last time," says my mother, "when they had to bomb the blockhouse on the coast." And we all go back to bed.

Mama goes to sleep right away. But I sit on my bed and continue to study the rectangle of cloudless night carved out by the window. The need to sleep slowly overwhelms me, but my eyes remain wide open. It is in this sort of half sleep that I begin to see fantastic shadows, somber shapes against the clear blackness of the sky. Like big black umbrellas, they rain down on the fields across the way, and then disappear behind the black line of the hedges.

No, I am not dreaming. Grandma was also not sleeping, and saw them from the window of the bedroom. I wake up Mama and my aunt. We hurriedly get dressed and go out into the courtyard. Once again, the sky is filled with a continuous, ever-intensifying hum. The hedgerows are alive with a strange crackling sound.[1] Monsieur Dumont, the neighbor across the street, a widower who lives with his three children, has also come out of his house. He comes toward us and shows me, hanging on the edge of the roof courtyard, a parachute. The Dumont kids follow their father and join us in the school courtyard. But the night has not yet revealed its secret.

An impatient curiosity is stronger than the fear that grips me. I leave the courtyard and make my way onto the road. At the fence of a neighboring field, a man is sitting on the edge of the embankment. He is harnessed with big bags and armed from head to foot: rifle, pistol, and some sort of knife. He makes a sign for me to approach him. In English I ask him if his plane was shot down. He negates that and in a low voice shoots back the incredible news: "It's the big invasion. . . . Thousands and thousands of paratroopers are landing in this countryside tonight." His French is excellent. "I am an American soldier, but I speak your language well; my mother is a Frenchwoman of the Basse Pyrénées." . . . I ask him, "What is going on along the coast? Are there landings? And what about the

Germans?" I was babbling; my emotions were overwhelming my thoughts. Ignoring my questions, he asked me about the proximity of the enemy and its relative presence in the area. I reassured him: "There are no Germans here; the closest troops are stationed in Sainte-Mère-Église, almost two kilometers from here."

The American tells me he would like to look at his map in a place where the light of his electrical torch will not be easily spotted. I propose that he come inside our house. He hesitates because he fears, he says, in the event that the Germans unexpectedly appear, he will put us in danger. I insist and reassure him: "Monsieur Dumont and my old aunt are going to watch the area around the school, one in front and the other in back." Then the soldier follows us, limping; he explains to me that he sprained his ankle on landing. But he would not let me care for him; there are many things more important. . . . In the classroom, to which Grandmama, Mama, and the Dumont children follow us, he takes off one of his three or four satchels, tears off the sticky little bands that sealed it, and takes out the maps. He spreads one out on a desk; it is a map of the region. He asks me to show him his precise location. He is astonished to discover how far he is from his targets: the railway tracks and the little river called the Merderet bordering the Neuville swamp toward the west.[2] I show him the road to follow in order to arrive there, where he is supposed to meet his comrades. He looks at his watch. Without thinking, I do as well. It is 11:20 p.m. He folds up his map, removes any trace of his presence, and after taking some chocolate out of his pocket which he gives to the children, so flabbergasted they forget to eat, he leaves us. He is perfectly calm and self-controlled, but the hand I shake is a little sweaty and stiff. I wish him luck in a voice that tries to be cheerful. And he adds in English—so that only I can understand—"The days to come are going to be terrible. Good luck, mademoiselle, thank you, I will not forget you for the rest of my life." And he disappears like a vision in a dream.

Once again, the mystery of the night deepens. We stay outside waiting for who-knows-what, keeping our voices low. Suddenly, there is an extraordinary blaze of light. The horizon in the direction of the sea lights up as if reflecting an immense fire that has been lit over the ocean. The formidable growl of marine artillery can be heard even here, although muffled by and submerged in a multitude of other inchoate sounds. The black silhouettes of airplanes arrive in the clouds and turn around in the sky. One of them passes just above our little school; it puts on its lights and releases . . . what? For an instant, we think it's a stick of bombs. But we are only starting to throw ourselves on the ground when parachutes open and float down like a mass of bubbles in the clear night. Then they scatter before disappearing in the confusion of the nocturnal countryside.

Another airplane passes over and releases its cargo. At first, the parachutes seem carried by the wake of the plane; then they drop vertiginously downward; finally the silk domes open. The descent gets slower and slower as they approach the ground. Those men whose dangling legs can clearly be seen get there a little more rapidly than those who hold bags of foodstuffs, equipment, ammunition. In a few moments, the sky is nothing more than an immense ballet of parachutes.

The spectacle on the earth is no less extraordinary. From all corners of the countryside shoot bursts of multicolored rockets as if thrown by invisible jugglers. In the fields all around us, big black planes slide silently toward the earth. Like flying Dutchmen, they land as if in a dream. These are the first groups of gliders. Our parachutist had been part of a group of scouts sent to signal the descent and landing zones.[3]

"SOMETHING UNUSUAL IS GOING ON"

The French had been waiting for days, months, years. No one knew the timing or the location of the invasion, but everyone had an opinion on those questions. There had been several false alarms, most famously the disaster in Dieppe in 1942. A small town on the northern coast of France, Dieppe was the site of an Allied invasion on August 19, 1942. On this day, a mostly Canadian force landed with the goal of occupying the town and luring the German Luftwaffe, or air force, into battle. Not only did the landings fail, but the Allies suffered an estimated fourteen hundred deaths.

Normans hoped that this time the landings would be different. Throughout the spring of 1944, the invasion was considered imminent. Yet it never came. As a result, people began to lose faith that the Allies would ever land. When the *débarquement* finally did occur, many Normans struggled to believe that it was actually taking place. Bernard Gourbin's account of the morning demonstrates just how hard it was to accept that the great day had finally arrived. An adolescent at the time, Gourbin lived with his family in the village of Ferté-Macé, southeast of Caen. Although close enough to the battle to hear it clearly, the villagers would have to wait until August 14 to be liberated.

It began a few minutes before midnight: a muffled, continuous noise. Difficult to sleep in such conditions. *Thunder*, my mother thought, as she struggled in vain to stay in her first deep sleep of the night. The muffled noise lasted until 8:30 a.m. At first, I heard nothing. Being in the fourth month of my fifteenth year, I always slept soundly. But the prolonged rumbling quickly woke me up. Even after a few minutes, my parents and I were still unable to close our eyes. So we began to talk to each other from our respective rooms, their doors half-open.

"Something unusual is going on," said my mother.

"What if they have landed?" I replied, noting that the noise was coming from the Nord, Falaise and Caen.[4]

My father agreed. "They've been telling us for weeks they were coming; eventually they have to arrive," he remarked self-assuredly.

In the street, people started to appear, their faces swollen for lack of sleep. They let out whoops of joy.

"They have landed!" declared the enthusiasts.

"Do you really think so?" replied the skeptics.

"Absolutely. I heard it on my radio."

"Perhaps you misunderstood," responded the disbelievers. "If they had really landed, that would have made still another uproar!"

In fact, my mother had been right. Something unusual and yet very real had happened. At 12:30 p.m., the BBC confirmed it. At 6:00 p.m., de Gaulle declared that "the Battle of France is engaged." After four years of occupation, it was hard for us to believe. And it was happening in our own backyard, yes, right here in Normandy! The thunder was, in fact, bombs and artillery, which had been pounding the coast—our coast—all night.[5]

* * *

Cécile Armagnac also found herself incredulous on the morning of the sixth. At the time, she was driving an ambulance with the Red Cross in Cherbourg. Like everyone else in this town at the northern tip of the Cotentin Peninsula, she had been unable to sleep because of the noise of the bombing. When the next morning she tried to phone her superiors in Paris, she was unable to get through. Telephone lines were down all over northern France, because both the Germans and the Resistance had been disabling the telephone network. But Armagnac was in for an even bigger surprise.

1:20 a.m. Alert; ended 1:30 a.m.[6]

2:45 a.m. Another alert; ended at 7:30 a.m.! Throughout the period, unusual noises: repeated and significant groups of airplanes passing over toward the east; machine gunning and anti-aircraft fire close by; uninterrupted droning and humming toward the distant south; muffled rumbling—perhaps bombs; a halo of light, not unlike at dawn, in the direction of the bay du Grand Vey.[7] Distant flashes and streams of light from the same direction. Several times, we three found ourselves on the terrace trying to figure out what was going on. Apparently, nothing in the immediate proximity of Cherbourg, and no call for an ambulance.

7:30 a.m. As soon as the alert ends, I call the post office to put through a call to the rue Octave-Feuillet in Paris. The operator responds:

"An indefinite wait, mademoiselle; it's impossible to reach Paris at the moment. Will you hold the call?"

"But it's important, even urgent! If you can't get through via Caen, could you try Rennes?"

"I have already tried for the *sous-préfecture*; it didn't work."

"Okay, please hold on to the number and call me as soon as you get it."

"I believe you will have to wait a long time! Don't you know the news? It appears that the Americans and English landed last night."

"Oh, sure . . . how long have we been waiting for that?!"

"I agree, but this time it happens to be true: the invasion is taking place between Caen and Sainte-Mère-Église . . . they're saying that the entire southern part of the region has been cut off."

"Not possible! Are you sure?"

"That's what I was just told! In any case, for the moment I can't even get through to Saint-Lô."

"Well, that really is a piece of news! The Cotentin isolated from the rest of the world? . . . I will call you again in an hour to see if that is still the situation."

It was, in fact, true. The *débarquement*, this myth so greatly hoped for and awaited during four long years, had in fact taken place that night. The *presqu'île de la Manche*[8] was indeed cut off from the continent, occupied and defended by the Germans, our enemies; bombed and invaded by the Americans, our allies — as fantastic and paradoxical as that situation might seem to be. . . . As for we three ambulance drivers in Cherbourg, we found ourselves penniless and cut off from our administration and all the other drivers . . . and for how much time?[9]

* * *

Like so many other people, Suzanne Bigeon, a nurse at a hospital in Cherbourg, confirmed the news of the landings by listening to the radio. Even if someone didn't own a radio, someone else in the neighborhood did. Bigeon's account suggests not only that many people did not believe in the landings, but also that not everyone was thrilled when they came.

People no longer really believed the landings would happen. The day before June 6, my block chief said to me in a discouraged tone: "Do you really believe in the landings?" Despite my own doubts, I put up a good show: "Absolutely, they will come." And he treated me like a crazy person.

The evening of the fifth of June at sunset—and by the way, I don't agree with those who say the Germans did not know what was going on—the sky in the Val de Saire lit up with orange rockets.[10] The number of alerts that night was impressive. I went to the window, since no one could sleep, and I saw armed German soldiers marching single file alongside the houses, crouching so as not to be seen. Simple coincidence?

The morning of June 6, we heard the distant bombing, which never seemed to end. The radio, camouflaged in the armoire in our living room, informed us of the landings, but also of the destruction of Valognes and Saint-Lô. This caused a great deal of consternation, because many parents and friends were refuged there, for the very purpose of avoiding the bombings. . . .

When I went to do errands, those who remained in the city, after having called out to the Americans for help for many years, were now almost hostile: "They are killing civilians; there is no more work, and no more money. They should either hurry it up or go away altogether!"[11]

Bigeon and her family were surprised to hear that Valognes and Saint-Lô were bombed, because Normandy generally had been spared bombing in the weeks just before the invasion. In response, many refugees from Paris and other cities had moved to the area for safety.[12]

Doubt about the *débarquement* was even more common in areas farther away from the coast. Here the radio was the only reliable source of information. Twenty-year-old Michel Béchet's diary reveals what the day of the landings was like for people farther south in Gorron, near Rennes.

Tuesday, June 6, 1944

The Allies have landed! The news began to circulate as early as this morning, but at first I could not believe it. For four years, we have been promised this day; for four years every good Frenchman from Normandy to Alsace has impatiently awaited it. While London, New York, and those who represent free France all proclaim that the famous "D" day has finally arrived, I—and many others— remain incredulous! No! It's unbelievable that the landings happened today, simply because it is too beautiful to be true. However, the news has been spread by persons who were able to hear it on the radio early this morning.

I say "early this morning" because for several days, our electricity has been cut off. Only for a very short period in the morning, at noon, and in the evening do we have a little power. Throughout the morning, then, everyone waited impatiently for noon to listen to London. Noon came and went, but the electricity did not come back. So instead there was idle chatter. It appears that the Allies have landed in the Nord and Normandy. Everyone is holding their breath. There are still many who are incredulous, but in general the people of Gorron believe that the landings have indeed taken place. Something extraordinary hangs in the air, and there is a sense that today is not like any other. No doubt that is the result of all the gossip in the town—the chitchat taking place on every corner. Who knows, but I do feel my heart fill suddenly with joy. Yes, this day could be one that will decide the destiny of France.

5:30 p.m. Counter to custom, the electricity and lights finally go on, and we have a chance to turn on our radios. Those who don't have one go to a friend or neighbor's house, where they listen, their hearts in their throats, as the rumors circulating since this morning are finally confirmed. "The landings took place last night," declares the speaker. There is fighting in the streets of Caen, and . . . good news! . . . According to the dispatches coming from London, the Allies are not meeting the resistance they expected.

Hundreds and hundreds of airplanes pass over Gorron. They are Flying Fortresses, and they cause large crowds of people to gather in the street in order to see these large flocks of giant birds.[13] Some people think they see parachutists being released. There's doubt about that, but one thing is for sure: there are bombardments; you can hear them really well from here.[14]

Like many Normans, Béchet was getting false information. It would be weeks before the Allies reached the city of Caen. The Germans had been told by Hitler to fight to the last man.

THE ANGUISH OF IGNORANCE

As Béchet's misinformation reveals, it was difficult to get reliable news in Normandy. And when civilians finally began to believe that the Allies were, in fact, landing, they had a set of burning questions: What was going on? Were the Allies winning or losing? Where were they? Most Normans had family members elsewhere in the region and were worried about their safety and whereabouts. With one's home and family at stake, figuring out what was happening was an urgent matter.

The German occupiers controlled the newspapers and forbade Normans from listening to foreign radio stations such as the BBC. When left to their own devices, civilians tried to figure out the course of events by interpreting sights and sounds. Thousands set their eyes toward the north and the glowing sky of the Cotentin coast. In the absence of other news, rumors began to spread throughout the region. Antoine Anne describes how word of the landings got around in his village of Saint-Georges-d'Elle, northeast of Saint-Lô.

On the night of June 5–6, we were awakened by a muffled rumbling; the earth was trembling. By the early morning hours, everyone was on the alert, rumors were flying, and the good news was spreading from mouth to ear: "It's the landings!" Our aim was to rediscover our freedom and dignity so that the servitude we had endured would no longer be anything but a bad memory. There are costs to resurrecting freedom. Our village, after the Liberation, had the sad privilege of being called the "capitol of ruins." For sure, people were nervous. After all, we had been waiting for this moment for a while. Everyone had their own prognosis. The question on everyone's lips was: what was going to happen? No one could really answer. Instead, we made reference to the old adage "You can't make an omelette without breaking eggs."[15]

World War I veterans, many now elderly men, were skilled interpreters of war sounds. Marcel Leveel's account of D-Day, based on diaries he had kept at the time, recounts an increasing storm of noise on the morning of June 6, and the efforts of veterans to detect its nature based on their experience at the Battle of Verdun. Nineteen years old in 1944, Leveel lived in Moon-sur-Elle, about ten miles north of Saint-Lô.

I awaken with a start and seem to be hallucinating. The noise I hear sounds like the clicking of castanets; the shaking house rattles the badly joined windows and doors. A tremendous, faraway noise overwhelms us. Something never before heard or experienced is happening here and now. . . . Constant thundering and explosions swallow up everything into a roar so immense you cannot identify any one sound. At first, I try to figure out from what direction it is coming. From inside my room, that proves to be impossible. I put on my glasses (always my first gesture when I get up), and I jump out of bed. At just this moment, Léon Barey opens the door and bursts in with a gust of wind:

"Get up right now! The situation is deteriorating, and I have the feeling it's going to get even worse. It is six o'clock. We've been hearing explosions along the coast since dawn a half hour ago. As usual, nothing serious, but in the last two minutes it's gotten really hellish. You can't stay here. Everyone in Le Rachinet has decided to leave.[16] Unlike here, the road is calm. There is no one in sight."

I leave the house. The sky is overcast, the day somber, and the weather cool. Outside, it is easier to figure out the location of the bombing. It is coming from the direction of the sea, no doubt along the coast, several dozen kilometers away. I am not able to distinguish between the detonations. For a long time, they come regularly and with the same intensity.

The Chemin de la Corde group[17] comes back. All together in the garden on the side of the road, with our faces turned north, we try to figure out what is going on. The veterans of 14/18 said it was definitely marine artillery from what had to be very large guns. It resembles Verdun except for the fact that airplanes are also attacking, big bombers which come to turn around above our heads. They are flying low, hidden by clouds so we can't see them. In the general din, we can barely hear them.[18]

A MIX OF MEANINGS

While everyone in Normandy awaited the invasion, what it meant for an individual depended on who he or she was—an optimist or a pessimist? A resistor or a collaborator? A child or an adult? Yvette Moreau was a little girl of eight years at the time of the landing, living with her family in Caen. She remembers the day—and the whole business of the *débarquement*—as an adult mystery. Nevertheless, she keenly observed how various types of people responded differently to the news.[19]

Tuesday, June 6, 1944

It was announced like the birth of a child, with that same mix of happiness and worry that accompanies the miracle of life. We awaited the Liberation just as a young woman awaits her first child—torn between impatience for a course of action she does not yet understand, and fear that it will actually take place. Like her again, we knew very well that neither haste nor apprehension could change the hour of our meeting.

They were going to land. On that everyone agreed. But where? When? How? Opinions strongly differed on these uncertainties.

Some thought, *What happiness!* The hour of victory approaches. The most difficult task will be to get a strong foothold on the coast. Then the towns will fall—one after the other. The way has been well prepared; the Germans seem weary. Let's have at them!

But those less optimistic—and no doubt more clear-eyed—insisted: "It's going to be hard going! You will see! We've never been able to beat them, and now they are very well settled here, as well as on their guard. Have you had a look at their artillery? They're not going to allow that to happen."

While there were opposing views, depending on individual temperament, everyone shared the hope that the landings would take place elsewhere. Farther north, in the Nord, of course! As far away as possible. In the meanwhile, they consolidated the shelters and hoarded their meager provisions: you never know!

Only those who sympathized with the occupying powers neglected such risky preparations. They allowed their present well-being to convince them of a similar utopia in the future. Nothing reassured them more than German sarcasm concerning our "futile" waiting: "Will they land? . . . will they not land?"

As for the Resistants, already harshly tested by the losses they had suffered in increasing numbers, they began to find the wait unbearable. Each morning came news of novel anxieties and sufferings. In their exhaustion they cried out: "What exactly are we waiting for?" Impatient to throw themselves into the final battle, they didn't care how it started. . . .

One word alone seemed to answer all our questions: "*débarquement.*" It was a new word for us, one that permeated all our conversations. Without really knowing its meaning, we found in it a response—a confused response—but a response nevertheless. If only it were associated with other words more at our level! We heard nothing but "German defeat" and "English victory," "ordeal and deliverance," "engagement," and "debacle," expressions very difficult for children of our age. There were other, more familiar words—"shelter," "bombardment," "supply"—which also figured there, as well as some virtues: "patience," "courage." From all this we learned only grief and confusion. This "*débarquement*" remained a vague and threatening phenomenon.

Without a doubt, its shadow hovered everywhere. Even in church on this first Sunday in June, it stole in to create an atmosphere of passionate fervor and supplication. The sermon had the grave tone of a solemn occasion, a little like the inflamed speeches that send troops into battle. But with us it left the same question: what exactly is a *débarquement*?

And then on the morning of June 6, 1944, we quickly caught on to the meaning of what we ourselves were living.[20]

As Moreau remarks, those who had collaborated with the Germans denied the very reality of the Liberation, which would mean reprisals against them. Still other collaborators made a show of excitement on the sixth of June, as Charles de la Morandière notices in the town of Granville along the western coast of the Cotentin.

On Tuesday, the sixth of June, around ten o'clock in the morning, one of my friends came to let me know that the English radio had announced the landings of Allied troops in the north of France. All night, airplanes had flown over the town in quite large squadrons; they seemed to be headed toward the south. Definitely English or American planes, because the German anti-artillery [DCA] had begun to fire, and toward the morning, the warning siren had gone off.

On all the walls outside, you could read large posters bordered in red, giving instructions in both German and French. From now on, no more going out after sunset, no groups of more than three persons, no more motorcycles, cars, no more restaurants or cafés. . . .

The inhabitants were almost open in showing their happiness. Joy shone on their faces, they shook hands with a funny little wink of the eye. Finally, the great day is here! The pro-Germans appear to be as delighted as the others. It's as if a wind of enthusiasm had swept away all hesitation and doubt. The announcement of the landings, which so many people have refused to believe out of ignorance, interest, or calculation, has purified the atmosphere.[21]

In contrast to collaborators, Resistance fighters saw the landings as an opportunity for action and revenge. For Jacqueline Sabine and her family in Caen, that revenge was extremely personal, fueled by loss as much as politics. Unlike others, the Sabines were eager to fight the war on their own property.

On Monday the fifth in the evening, we had all gone to bed and were sleeping when, in the middle of the night, we were awakened by a powerful rumbling. Not simply a local bombardment, it was instead a constant roar, coming from the north in the direction of the sea.

We were overwhelmed, happy, and worried all at once: finally it was the landings, and so close to Caen, right on our own Calvados coast!

Ah! If only the maps got through to London via Jean Midiaux's network! They show where the Germans have placed machine guns on the minor roads in the forbidden zone. I was able to pass them over, hidden inside the covers of my Latin book — with private lessons being the pretext. My father, a technician at the electrical factory, had a pass to travel to farms on the plains north of town not far from the sea; he was able to verify the installations. Using his excellent visual and topographical memory, he drew what he noticed while circulating on bicycle. The information could help Allied airplanes to avoid anti-aircraft fire. This was our humble way of responding to the cruel deportation of our Jacques, a student at Malherbe high school, who was not even seventeen years old at the time of his transfer from Caen to Germany in May of 1943. He would be eighteen on June 18, 1944.[22]

Some members of the Resistance saw the landings as the difference between life and death. On June 6, Resistance member Jean Roger was living in Saint-Lô, awaiting orders to participate in the battle and in danger of arrest at any moment.[23] Roger suggests another way the Normans confirmed that the invasion had indeed taken place: the panicky behavior of the Germans and the presence of American prisoners of war.

I am going to be twenty-three on the second of August. I am an unimportant member of the Resistance (OCM) awaiting instructions to participate more actively in the war effort.[24] In the meanwhile, I have yet to recover from a terrible scare: some days before, my network was seriously infiltrated. Dufour came to my office in order to arrest my direct superior, Monsieur Deffes.[25] The affair is not over, and I have yet to be reassured of my own safety. So I and many others have an additional reason to anticipate the landings with great impatience. . . .

On the sixth of June around 5:00 a.m., I am awakened by an enormous boom, a sort of cannon firing without end—a ceaseless storm. A glow on the horizon seems to be coming from the direction of the east coast. My parents wake up. The diagnosis is rapid: "they" are arriving! We are on the lookout at the windows for the rest of the night. Our crazy hopes are finally taking form. The first news bulletins broadcast the messages of Roosevelt, Eisenhower, and de Gaulle.[26] I am overwhelmed with a feeling of joy as well as expectation. In a matter of hours or at most days, the Dufours of the world are going to pay. Our humiliation was coming to an end. Yes, it was the most beautiful day of my life. The prisoners, the rations, the collaborators, the sirens, the bombings, the Gestapo, Hitler and his team of gangsters . . . order was going to be rapidly restored. The hour of revenge had sounded.

At the time, it never even occurred to me that the landings might actually fail.

From the window of our apartment, situated on the third floor, 3 rue de la Poterie, I glance at Feldkommandatur 722, which is about twenty-five meters away in the back of a small square facing the rue Dame-Denise.[27] The news is confirmed. You can see signs of a great concern beginning to operate there. Numerous military vehicles arrive and leave; suitcases are stacked up inside the cars. This panicky departure fills me with joy.

In order to witness the events close up, I go downstairs. Suddenly, I see a German car arriving at the Kommandatur. It is filled with soldiers dressed in khaki, their faces smeared in black. They are heavily guarded by German soldiers, and we guess that these prisoners are the first American parachutists being led to an interrogation. As discreetly as possible, I try to wink in their direction in order to assure them of my sympathy in this difficult moment. They appear to me to be tired and withdrawn.

My friends and I spend the day traveling through the town attempting to get the latest information, all while hearing reports from London and trying to see if the Germans were speeding up their preparations to depart. You had to spy on the occupants without seeming to provoke them, given that their anger could be dangerous. Wounded wildcats can be fearsome. In the course of our "patrols," we pass in front of the prison. Have our imprisoned friends heard "the news"? We feel that they should celebrate even more than us, despite their being anxious about the immediate future.

No German airplane to be seen. When will the Allies arrive? It seems to us that we could debate the day, the hour, but not the actual fact of their arrival. We have already begun to put together plans for their welcome . . . provided that everything goes okay![28]

HOPEFUL OPTIMISM

Jean Roger was not the only optimist in Normandy. Hopes ran high; the Allied army was admired. Many Normans believed that the battle would take hours, at most days. The Germans proved them wrong, of course. Still, people believed. The diary of J. de Saint-

Jorre gives us an example of Norman confidence in the Allies. In retrospect, de Saint-Jorre's belief that the city of Saint-Lô would welcome the Americans on D-Day seems both naïve and ironic. In fact, that battle for Saint-Lô would rage until July 19; bombing would leave the city in ruins. Despite his optimism, however, de Saint-Jorre knew enough to take precautions: he sent his family south to a shelter.

Tuesday, June 6

After a bad night, Saint-Lô awakens, troubled by an immense hope. The Germans hastily pack their bags; the officers' mess is moving, and transport services load heavy trucks with baggage and documents. I go in search of news. It is not yet seven o'clock in the morning, but already everyone is up and out. "What's going on?" people cry out to each other. An orderly in the Passive Defense yells to me in passing: "They're here! They've landed!" Joy appears on faces wrenched by emotion and sleeplessness. When German vehicles pass by, an ironic smile appears on everyone's lips. "Finally they are leaving!" For an instant, everyone believes that the Germans are going to leave without fighting, and that tomorrow, perhaps even this evening, the Americans will make their triumphal entry into Saint-Lô. That seems possible, since the landings would be taking place only twenty kilometers from the town.

At 7:00 a.m., after having considered the risks of the situation, I decided to send my family to a shelter in a small locality south of Saint-Lô.

In town, the spectacle is curious. Everywhere the Germans are running around with their horse rigging, loading their suitcases in cars camouflaged with branches. The German military Command and Tribunal are emptying out. Soon the Germans bring out bundles of bilingual posters, in black with a red border, for immediate distribution. They announce exceptional measures, restrictions on movement, curfews, roundups. No means of transportation is working. Every hour, light bombers pass over at a low altitude, flying over roads like hornets, in search of a convoy to machine gun. The sirens blare several times during the day, but no one pays attention to them. The news circulates, distorted by feverish imaginations.[29]

The citizens of Caen were also optimistic, although again such confidence was misguided. Caen was one of the first objectives of the British and Canadian divisions in the Normandy Invasion. It took weeks for that city to fall, and like Saint-Lô it was almost completely destroyed by bombing. Madame Hardouin relates the high hopes raised by the landings east of the Cotentin Peninsula. She was only eleven years old in 1944, and so gives us a unique child's view of the morning of June 6. Her mother shrewdly used all her ration tickets that morning to buy bread. Soon, the Hardouins would be forced to leave their home, which was completely destroyed in the battle.

A constant distant rumbling insults my ears and permeates my brain. A roar—indistinct, obsessive, exasperating, ghostly—is cradling my dreams. Two days ago I had my First Communion, and despite all the restrictions, my parents made it a joyous occasion. Now in my half sleep, I am still dreaming of it. At eleven years old, I would not easily awaken even if lightning struck my bed. I wander in a fog of sleep.

The house seems empty, but the street outside is lively. What is this medley of voices I hear at such an early hour? It is not even 6:00 a.m. yet; they must be crazy ... I turn over and go back to sleep; I still have time before going to school.

But the rumble does not stop, and the earth starts trembling, shaking the windows. What a fantastic storm! The murmur of voices, at first low and incomprehensible, now becomes more intensive, scheming. I hear little snatches of conversation: "No doubt about it, it's them." Mama appears in the doorway: "Sleep . . . they are landing." An exclamation of joy rather than anguish. My spirits brighten. . . .

Mama makes another brief appearance: "I'm going to the bakery . . ." And then she is out of the house. I'm left with a thousand questions. It is 6:30 a.m.; she has never done errands this early. Something is definitely wrong. Shivering, I get dressed and go out into the street, now humming with people from our neighborhood. I find Papa talking with a friend and listen in: "This time, it's really them! We've been waiting such a long time! . . . No doubt about it, they've come to liberate us." I've understood, but who is "they"? Surely it's the English. I am always hearing talk of the English radio, which papa secretly goes to hear at his friend Legac's house. My father sees me: "Let's go inside again. Rumor has it that the Krauts are rounding up able-bodied men."

Mama doesn't come back from the bakery; evidently there's a long line . . . and what if her wait inside is even longer? Outside, it is still rumbling.

"They are going to pass through here. Apparently they are in the Lébisey woods. This evening they will liberate us; there are only a few Germans in Caen," said Papa in an optimistic tone. I am reassured. But all the same, what if the war lasts longer? The Germans would be able to cut off our water in order to harm us . . . "I am going to fill my empty barrel with three hundred liters of water—enough for the whole neighborhood," announces the master of the house.

Luckily, he is home. Yesterday he was supposed to conduct a train to Paris, but a friend discouraged him from leaving: "Stay here, Louis, tomorrow is going to be a big day." No other explanation. He hadn't really understood, but made his own suppositions and followed this man's advice.

Mama finally comes back, her arms full of gray bread. Oh, my God, she used all her rationing tickets at once . . .

"Mama, it's time to go to school; I am going to be late."

"Stay here."

"But I am going to get in trouble!"

"It's more sensible for you to stay here and wait to see what happens!"[30]

SEEING THE INVASION

Normans living on the coast in the landing areas could see as well as hear the invasion. Some were witness to the light effects of artillery, which illuminated the sky with an eerie beauty. Still others watched in astonishment as the Allies unleashed their formidable naval force. Thousands upon thousands of vessels crossed the English Channel on D-Day morning. From Caen, the view of the invasion was spectacular, as Danièle Philippe remembers. Born at Molay-Littry near Omaha Beach, Philippe was fifteen years old on June 6, when she and her mother, her sister, Colette, and her brother, Michel, all found themselves with a front-row seat on the invasion from the window of their attic.

> Around 11:00 p.m. we finally decided to go to sleep, but shortly after midnight we were awakened with a start by the crash of thunder. Bombs were exploding very near to where we were. Airplanes were hedge-hopping. German anti-aircraft artillery was firing nonstop. It crackled from every direction and made a terrible racket. . . . We couldn't see much from the windows on the first floor. On the second floor, the trees got in the way. So we got the idea of going to the attic. From that height we could put our heads outside by opening the dormer window as much as possible. But we were all too little—even Mama. Michel went to get the footstool from the bathroom, while the strange glow of the storm lit up the attic. Mama moved the window out to its last notch. After having taken a look around, she came down from the stool, absolutely

horrified. Colette, also rendered speechless, abandoned the place I demanded. It was indeed hallucinatory. A phantasmagorical night! I fell into a stupor, but Michel tugged me on the sleeve. One after another, we took our turns in the dormer opening, almost fighting with each other in order to profit from the unbelievable view above the roofs.

The sky was ablaze with intense light and seemed to be toppling forward into a continuous wave of lanterns, flames, and stars. In the direction of the sea, an immense band of illumination closed the horizon. Still more powerful lights pierced this unreal brightness, dazzling and driving back the night. Some fires surprised us by remaining fixed in this moving world. They hung on as if hitched to the sky, then disappeared all at once. The luminous beams of the searchlights probed the night, sweeping the sky toward us, crossing as if to search each other. The passing lights sparkled white and red. The night was alive, unreal, magnificently and terribly beautiful.[31]

Still another amazing sight that morning was the vision of the Allied armada making its way across the channel. By far the largest fleet ever assembled, it contained 5,000 landing ships, including 6 battleships, 23 cruisers, 104 destroyers, and 152 escort vessels. British and American warships predominated, but were joined by Canadian, French, Polish, Dutch, and Norwegian vessels.[32] Pierre Ferrary and his wife, Yvonne, witnessed the landings from their home at Grandcamp-les-Bains, where Allied strength was on full display. Like many Normans, they were amazed—and reassured—by the extraordinary show of force made by the Allies that morning. The first sighting of the ships moved Normans beyond measure.

During the night of the fifth to the sixth of June, with our suitcases packed for this purpose, we are once again obliged to take cover in a ditch. From there we seem to hear an intense rumbling which, however distant, is new to our ears. There are no planes flying overhead, so what is this noise? We think it might be a cannon equipped with large pieces of artillery: is it the landings? . . . Then the airplanes arrive by hundreds, thousands. It's a formidable, almost inconceivable swarm, in a sky of fire. One bomb explosion follows another, and our young servant is sobbing out of fear. . . .

Then there is a brief calm. Maybe it's not the landings after all? That would be very disappointing for us. But then the bombing picks up again with growing intensity and continues until dawn, which finally arrives after an interminable night spent between two walls of earth at the bottom of a hole.

Scarcely had we drunk a bit of coffee when the neighborhood children rush up: "Mama says for you to come quickly to the garden with your binoculars to see the naval landing craft escorting the troops!"

So we all leave.

Upon seeing the spectacle before us, we are overwhelmed by emotion.

As far as the eye can see from the shores of the Cotentin in the west to the first promontory of cliff running east to Vierville, the sea is covered with hundreds and hundreds of vessels—cargo ships, barges, landing craft of all kinds and tonnage.

Rumors are already circulating the there are eight thousand ships in the bay. We have no idea; it is impossible to count them . . .

We throw ourselves in each other's arms; we embrace each other. Tears gather on our eyelashes; they run down my wife's cheeks. With all our senses we take in this extraordinary scene. We have waited for it day and night for four years, all while listening to our radio—often disappointed, never desperate, and always confident. It is D-Day and H-Hour. All our hopes are finally being realized![33]

CHAPTER TWO

THE *PARAS*

In the very first hours of the sixth of June, sleepy Normans rose from their beds to watch the war approaching from the English Channel. In planes above their heads sat men who could not be more wide awake. Not only were they getting thrown about the fuselage by the impact of German anti-aircraft fire, but they were about to jump out into a barrage of artillery and the danger of enemy territory. Luckily, the German Luftwaffe (air force) was nowhere to be seen. Three Allied divisions dropped into the darkness of France that night: the British 6th Airborne Division, and the American 82nd and 101st Airborne Divisions. Before dawn, eight thousand British and sixteen thousand American servicemen would parachute into Normandy.[1] The first to come were the British, who dropped shortly after midnight; the Americans followed about an hour later.

Their mission: to seize key towns, bridges, and waterways so as to cut off the Cotentin Peninsula from the rest of France. Dropped to the east, the British 6th was to secure the Orne River and the Caen Canal. Farther north and west, the American 82nd was to take the tiny town of Sainte-Mère-Église, where roads from every direction converged.[2] The 82nd was also instructed to capture bridges on the Merderet River so that the Americans could advance rapidly across, toward the southwest. Farther south, the American 101st was to seize bridges on the Douve River and also gain control of the locks and causeways leading from the sea to Carentan. Once the Germans were cut off from supplies and reinforcements, the GIs would march north to Cherbourg.

That was the plan, anyway. The drops were a different matter. The terrible fog made it impossible for pilots to navigate. No sooner were they over the channel than their planes were hit by German flak, causing them to panic and release their men either too early or too late. As a result, almost no one landed where they were supposed to have. Worse still, many planes were flying as low as four hundred or five hundred feet when they released their men. The paratroopers had very little time to open their chutes. Their impact with the ground broke their ankles and legs. Some men fractured their backs, becoming paralyzed, and still others landed with a dull thud, becoming the invasion's first casualties.

In Sainte-Mère-Église, sixteen-year-old Jeannette Pentecôte remembers a man confronting the dangers of a low jump.

When I raised my head, I saw a transport plane skimming the roofs of the village and passing over my house. The plane was flying so low that I could very clearly distinguish its wide-open door on the side. In its frame stood a paratrooper who was ready to jump into the void, but who seemed surprised by the meager height from which he had to jump. To this day I remember this paratrooper's face as he prepared to jump and was stunned to find himself so low.[3]

SUSPICION AND FEAR

By three o'clock in the morning on the sixth of June, little bands of soldiers were wandering everywhere on the peninsula, separated from one another and miles from where they were supposed to be. Hundreds were not only lost but also unable to walk. Meanwhile, civilians in Sainte-Mère-Église were waking up and realizing that a quiet nocturnal invasion had taken place. Here is how Odette

Eudes, thirteen years old at the time, remembers D-Day in this small town. Like other Normans, she calls the paratroopers *paras*. Despite her fear, she was struck by the beauty of the 82nd Airborne falling through the night sky.

About twelve days before the landings, we were up several times during the night, because planes were passing over and we could see lights over Cherbourg. We went to bed fully dressed just in case. Then after a period of calm, the same thing happened again on the night of June 5–6.

Our group consisted of my parents and we four children, the Levesque family (four persons), and Madame Rioult and her two children. Monsieur Rioult didn't want to get up for what he thought was a false alarm. We went to the house of Monsieur and Madame Flamand and their daughter Cécile, a family living on the other side of the courtyard. We were all in the kitchen, forbidden to speak and respond if someone knocked on the door (which did happen later). At the moment when the planes released their cargo of paratroopers, Papa and I looked out a small window, about forty millimeters square. It was truly magical to see all the paratroopers descend from the sky.

The Americans touched down and as quickly as possible released themselves from their harnesses. Bent over with their guns at the ready, they ran alongside the wall bordering the house. Monsieur Rioult decided to join us after all (it was he who had knocked on the door). But no one responded. With the *paras* coming down everywhere, he dove into a ditch near the house. The soldiers held him at bay with their rifles. . . . When they realized he was French, they gave him a rod with a helmet at its end, and marched him some steps to Gallini's café. (When he finally joined us at noon, he was very pale because he had been so afraid.)

In the meanwhile, around 9:00 a.m., Papa and Monsieur Flamand left the house and went to see the soldiers. Among them was a wounded soldier who could not walk. Papa offered to put him on his back and walk with him up to the street, but the soldier refused, making Papa understand that if a German took a shot, both of them would be killed.[4]

As Eudes's account suggests, the first encounters between Americans and Normans were dances of suspicion and fear. Also in Sainte-Mère-Église that night, Maurice Mauger and his sister, Alice, awoke to see isolated soldiers not only miles from their destination but also injured from their landing.

At dawn, when we opened the door of our home, we saw that the canopy of a parachute was covering most of the garage roof. In a corner of the property, a *para* with a hostile expression was hidden in a bush, holding a machine gun in his hand. The man was groggy and seemed to be in shock from his rough landing. He was moving with difficulty. He pointed to the roof of the farm and made us understand that he had hit it, creating a hole in the slate before falling again heavily to the ground.

A few moments later, another *para* returned to the farm. He went to see our mother and asked her the location of the hamlet Loutres; he told her that this place was an assembly point for the Americans. Our mother, who was originally from Turqueville, had no trouble explaining precisely where the hamlet was located.[5] The grateful *para* gave her a package of cigarettes before disappearing.[6]

The Americans were suspicious of the French. Normans still remaining near the landing areas, they were told, were collaborators protected by the Germans. Property was to be thoroughly inspected for enemy troops who may be hiding there. As for the French, the sight of these American soldiers, with their arsenal of weapons and their blackened faces, proved terrifying. Sixteen-year-old Jean Flamand and his family, neighbors of Odette Eudes, were frozen with fear when a *para* landed in their garden. Flamand could not help noticing how much weaponry the man was carrying, including guns, knives, and ammunition.

The day of the fifth passed by without event; it was hot and sunny. At night, everyone slept in their own homes in order to resume their usual routine the next day. The moon shone brilliantly; the night sky was magnificent, studded with stars. We were sleeping soundly when around 11:00 p.m., we were awakened by the bell ringing in the old church. Anguish gripped us all. My parents got up; my father went out, looked out over the town, came back, and declared, "There is a fire in Sainte-Mère."

I got up, as did my sister. Behind the church, we could see an enormous red and orange glow shooting up into the sky. It was the house of Mademoiselle Pommier . . . which was on fire. Everyone in the hamlet was outside. We had been standing on the steps to the door for several minutes when we turned our eyes toward the coast. A rumbling sound grew nearer to us; my parents thought that a bombardment was imminent. We went back inside. From the window of the house suddenly appeared a multitude of Dakota planes flying at low altitude and headed straight for Sainte-Mère-Église. They came by the hundreds, covering the sky with their big wings. Some pulled another plane behind them, and you could see the cord connecting them (these trailing planes were the gliders).[7] I could make out the fuselage of various machines and was struck dumb when suddenly I saw packages falling into the void. Abruptly ten, one hundred, one thousand parachutes opened, swinging in the air.

Each wave of planes unloaded their cargo of large red, white, green, and blue domes into the inferno of crackling machine-gun fire. Anti-artillery gunners fired on the paratroopers, who were unable to defend themselves as they flew down. Many of them fell to the ground, dead or mortally wounded. It was a sight I will never forget! I even saw a paratrooper fall right in the garden in front of our house. He landed in a row of garden peas, breaking the stakes. We watched without saying a word, dumbstruck, astonished, not knowing what was going to happen. Abruptly, the door opened and a man, his face blackened and his head covered with a khaki-net helmet, entered. It was a sight worthy of Dante, this black man from the sky.

I looked at him from head to foot, front and back; I looked at his legs and his arms. His uniform had many pockets, all filled to bursting. Around his waist were grenades and bullets. In his left hand he held a machine gun, and on his right leg was a sheath held by a leather lace, holding a dagger. . . . All of a sudden, we had become mute. He stared at us one after the other. I got closer to my father, and my sister stuck close to my mother's skirts. Abruptly, he raised his machine gun on us and made us understand that we were not to make a move. We were overcome with fear.

He moved forward, searched the house, opened the furniture, and looked everywhere. Then he once more approached us, but now he began to smile, speaking to us in English. On the fifth of June, 1944, at 11:30 p.m., we were all smoking an Old Gold, our first American cigarette, and also sizing up chewing gum, a kind of candy that was unknown to us, but which this man took out of many of his pockets. Then with a movement of his hand, he said good-bye, then came back once more and said in broken French: "Okay, don't be afraid, it's the landings!" With that he disappeared into the night.

My father's first reaction was to say: "Well well, he speaks French!"[8]

RESCUING, HEALING, EVACUATING

Paras who were severely injured or lost had no option but to trust the French. After having had a paratrooper fall in the family garden in Sainte-Mère-Église, Flamand found many other *paras* in a field nearby. He and his family cared for them as best they could.

The parachutes we recovered were resting on a green and luxuriant meadow between our house and the Vallée de Misère. Eventually, the silk of these parachutes would serve to make corsages, blouses, shirts for us to use as clothing. We weren't rich, and to wear such soft and silky clothes seemed to us to be a luxury we would otherwise never be able to give ourselves. When we went to look for one of these parachutes, we ended up on the other side of the hedge, where something gave us a start. Lying on his side, in the grass under the hedge, a paratrooper seemed to be sleeping. We approached him. The man was visibly in terrible pain. He would moan every time he made a movement. He did not let go of his gun, which rested in his hand. Because he could not walk, my parents tried to pick him up in order to bring him to the house. He must have been there since 11:30 p.m. the night before, awaiting either help or death.

On his hands and feet, with our help, he was able to get to our house where my mother gave him something to drink, brought him a chair so we could sit him down. He suffered more and more. Several of his comrades, who were alerted by my father, came to look for him and bring him back in a jeep which had been parachuted down, and which was circulating on Highway 13. We guessed that he had fallen into the trees and had fractured his vertebral column. When he was upright, he looked out of joint, like a jumping jack. What became of him? Did death deliver him from his suffering? Did he remain ill? We will probably never know.[9]

Many Normans were left with such questions. Flamand's family's use of the parachute silk was very common. In the next few years, hundreds of Norman brides would be married in dresses made from that material.

Several miles south of Sainte-Mére-Eglise, in the small town of Rémilly-sur-Lozon, a Resistance fighter paid the ultimate price for his attempt to evacuate wounded paratroopers to safety. His widow tells the story.

On June 7, my husband told me, "I saw paratroopers in the village of L'Abbaye.[10] They asked me if there were Germans in Rémilly. Since there were only a few there at the time, I said no." Upon hearing that, the paratroopers sent a messenger pigeon and said that it wouldn't be necessary to bomb Rémilly—that was how our town was saved from air raids.

My husband would often travel to Gateaux to see Monsieur de Gouville, a member of Organisation Civile and Militaire, who would give him directives.[11] Once, after finding five English paratroopers, he hid them near Château de Montfort castle.[12] He later brought a group of six American paratroopers to join them. So in all, my husband took it upon himself to protect and provide supplies to eleven or twelve Allied soldiers.

The Germans soon caught wind of the paratroopers' presence at Château de Montfort. My husband decided to evacuate the soldiers, and found them a safe hiding place four kilometers away in Mesnil Eury. He went to get them during the night, taking the wounded man on his shoulders.

In the meanwhile on July 2, he had tried to blow up Bâteau Bridge on the road to Marchésieux. Someone had either let something slip or denounced him, because Germans began to keep an eye on him. For several days, a soldier had been sitting on a large rock on the corner of Monsieur Albert Lehodey's property, watching my husband's movements—although he didn't go out much, because he knew they were watching.

We had been staying with Madame Lemanissier, my grandmother, but when a shell landed close to the house and shattered all the windows, we decided to return to our home. When my husband went out to fetch the bedding, the Germans followed him and went into the garage. He saw them in the garage and went to see what they were doing. They gave the excuse that they had come to get some wood. After a brief conversation, one of the soldiers—who had planned all along to start a fight—began shouting threats. Then he took out his revolver and shot my husband straight in the heart, before the horrified eyes of Gabriel and Yves. My poor children ran back screaming, clinging to everyone in sight and telling them, "They killed Papa."[13]

Young Normans, too, rushed to help the *paras*, sometimes getting in way over their heads. Innocence led to tragedy. This was the case of a teenage boy named Bernard from a small village near Carentan. Marcel Jourdain tells Bernard's story.

The next day, in the afternoon, I left for the manor, in order to talk about the big events [the landings] with Bernard, and just to pass the time. . . . At the manor, Marguerite, Bernard's sister, dusted and polished as usual with a feather duster in her hand. She told me that I would not be able to see Bernard, that he was very busy. But no luck for her—at that very moment he came out of the kitchen, relaxed and in his slippers.

"*Salut*, old friend. Wow! The great day has arrived, and it is here where we live." He seemed extremely happy.

"Yes, it seems so."

Disturbed and upset by the trickery Marguerite had just used to get rid of me, I said nothing more. But it really made me wonder. It was not their style to be so offhanded with someone.

"So you are too busy, Marguerite told me; I'll leave."

"No, wait a minute."

[Bernard and Marguerite] made an exchange of glances. Then Bernard said to me rapidly, "Come on, follow me, move."

I followed him into the kitchen, where I was met with a surprise.

My feet were glued to the floor. In the half light at the back of the great room, a soldier with a hue the color of hay stared at me with a guarded look. The wounded man was stretched out in an armchair, his right leg and ankle wrapped and resting on a small stand.

"An American!"

"This is a young French friend," Bernard told him.

"French speak a little bit," said the American.

"Okay, now, shake his hand and say good-bye; he's not here to make small talk."

In the kitchen, Bernard made me promise to absolute secrecy, and told me how he had recovered this American *para* (his name was Bob) who was lost, isolated, and, worse still, crippled. Early in the morning, when Marguerite and her maid went out to do the milking, in a meadow on the edge of the moor, they heard a whistle. They thought someone was calling their dog. At the car, while they were transferring the milk from their buckets to the churns, the whistling started again, this time insistent. They thought it was a joke. Just to put their own minds to rest, however, they approached the hedge and passed down along it, giving it a good look. It was then that a head in a helmet, with a face covered in black and streaming morning dew, appeared to them from between two separated branches. Both cried out in fear and held on to each other.

"My soldier American. Bonjour you no fear. Germans here?"

"Yes, but they have left, all left."

Then Marguerite went to find Bernard.

Bernard could speak a little English. Once he arrived at the spot and gave a look all around him, he said in a low voice, "Friend French." . . . When the American told him with a grimace that he had smashed his ankle, Bernard backed the car up to the branches and helped him to haul himself on board between two rows of milk cans. He threw several jute sacks on top of him in order to cover him up completely. "Okay," said the American, smiling and grimacing at the same time. He must have been suffering from his ankle.

On the way back, the car ran into some German *paras* who were going toward Sainte-Mère or Carentan. The American, lying flat at the back of the car between the milk cans and across the side slats of the old jalopy, could see their faces, sometimes only a meter away. The swaying and bumping, combined with the effects of fatigue and pain, made him suddenly violently nauseous. Bernard heard him vomiting under the jute. Perhaps it was also the turmoil caused by seeing so near the faces of those he had the mission to kill . . .

With the car finally under way, Bernard helped him to sit up in the back. He took big breaths. A chill ran through his body. He was green and sick as a dog. Large drops of sweat beaded up on his forehead and cheeks. As they streamed down his face, they mixed with the morning dew and washed away some of his chimney-sweep makeup.

"And if he brings the Germans to your house?" I asked. No problem for Bernard. He told me that two had already come in a motorcycle, deputy officers. They were looking for a shed in order to shelter a cannon and tractor for the night. . . . When Bob heard the motorcycle and looked out the window, he saw them crossing the courtyard, and took out his pistol, ready to receive them.

"Aren't your parents afraid?" No problem there either. The Americans are landing on the coast by the thousands. They should arrive here en masse in a few days. Always so optimistic, Bernard. Much more than the other people of the village. Some of them were even asking themselves: and what if this is a new Dieppe?[14]

In fact, Jourdain had good reason to be worried. Bob was soon joined by more *paras*, who hid near Bernard's house. A few days later, as Bernard was trying to feed them, he was shot dead by a German.

Sometimes, entire villages worked together to care for wounded *paras* and help them rejoin the Allied lines. This was the case of the small village of Prétot, southwest of Sainte-Mère-Église. Michel Birette tells us the story of what happened. Twenty-one years old at

43

the time, Birette was in hiding, because he had refused the occupiers' demand that he go to Germany to do forced labor. Sheltered by a neighbor on that man's farm, he would soon be joined by several Americans.

The next day, the seventh of June, I discovered three wounded American *paras* hiding in a field close to the farm. The boys had fractures, mostly in their ribs and hips. With Pierre Huet, we went to get help, and we led them to the farm. We hid them upstairs in a room with two openings. It was in a sort of barn where one stored hay. You had to climb a ladder to get to the room. I stayed there with the wounded men for about seven or eight days. The leader of this group was called "Mike," and he stated that his men were supposed to go to Amfreville.[15] But they were in too poor a condition to be able to move, and at every moment risked being found by German patrols on the lookout for them. The mayor of Prétot at this time, Monsieur Lefevre, also hid a group of four *paras*. In the end, the men of the village consulted one another with the goal of gathering all the wounded men found in the territory of the commune. It was decided that the wounded found at Monsieur Lefevre's house should join the men found at the home of Monsieur Huet. In this way, the seven men met back up with one another at the farm. They took shelter in the room upstairs that served as a sort of barn. These *paras* were nice, but seemed resolved not to be captured without a fight in case the Germans broke in on them. On the floor of the room they had installed a machine gun, ammunition belts, and grenades. Every day I visited them, and when I could, I brought them food, chocolate, and provisions. The group of seven stayed several days, but were taken prisoner by the Germans only a few days before the liberation of Prétot.

Those *paras* in good health and hidden in Prétot were brought together through the cooperation of the village population. Some of them were hidden on a path near the farm of Pierre Huet, but also a little throughout the region of the commune. Isolated *paras* were also found on the coast of Vindefontaine. Then at the end of a few days, a human chain was formed to try to get the lost men across German lines so that they could rejoin the American forces. So it was that in the company of Pierre Huet and Roger Hauvel, I made night voyages on two or three occasions. These consisted of leading the American *paras* at night from Prétot to the farm of Monsieur Davazac in Vindefontaine, a building situated on the edge of the swamp. From there, ferrymen took charge of them, bringing them across the flooded marshes in a small boat.[16]

Paratroopers were not the only soldiers rescued by villages working in cooperation. Sometime in the first few days of the invasion, a Boeing B-17 Flying Fortress was gunned down by German anti-aircraft fire off the coast of Chausey, an island west of the Cotentin Peninsula. The Chausey community rescued, clothed, and hid the four pilots who survived the disaster. Edouard Marie, a fisherman on the island, tells the story.

Thick clouds of Flying Fortresses, those big bombers, cut across the sky: there are hundreds of them at one time. From our perch at the top of the fort, we can see German anti-aircraft firing without stopping. Despite the [German] prohibition from going out on the sea, Roland Vidament decides that we should go out at Minquiers in order to raise up our pots and shelter them from bad weather. So we leave around six or seven in a sailboat and a rowboat, with two dories in tow. It is the eighth of June; the sea is calm and the sky blue.

A mile out, off the last rocks of the archipelago which we had just passed, Roland's brother, Robert, turns around and sees several balls of fire fall on the island.

"They're bombing!" he cries.

Thinking of our wives and children, we turn around at full throttle in order to rejoin the group. We draw alongside the hold and learn that a Flying Fortress has just fallen in fire on the middle of the island after having exploded in flight.

Four pilots who have jumped in their parachutes are recovered from the sea by fishermen remaining on the island: one is brought in by dinghy by Léopold G. Gosselin; another, seriously wounded in the head, brought in by Pierre Leperchoise; the last two found on a rock by Edouard Lapie in the area surrounding the *Conchée*. The wounded man is transported to the presbytery, where the priest, aided by women, does his best to care for him. Abbé Jourdan stitches up the wound with the poor means at his disposal.

Meanwhile, we go to the wreck of the plane, but the fire has not yet been put out, so no one can get too near—the munitions might explode. A fifth man is found charred in the cabin. Helped by Henri Le Guillerm, Louis Gosselin makes a coffin with some boards, and buries the poor unfortunate in the little cemetery of the island facing Port-Marie.

Because the weather is wonderful, with a blue, clear sky, we thought that the Germans in Granville had been able to see the paratroopers go down. . . . What are they going to do? While waiting, we need to deal with more pressing matters, such as finding dry clothing for these men. This is a problem, because the soldiers are big strapping fellows. Marie Leperchois had the clothes of her brother-in-law, Jean Batany, a Breton sailor who fished in Minquiers before the war. As a result of circumstances, he went back to his native province. In this way, the wounded pilot who took his clothes came to be named *Batany*. . . .

While awaiting events, the four Americans were sheltered at the hotel-restaurant of mother Madame Leperchois, who worked to feed them the best she could, with everyone helping her by bringing a bit of fish. There we are condemned to inaction on the island, without food, that is, without bread, without potatoes, without sugar, without "coffee" or rather, without grilled barley, since there hadn't been any real coffee for a long time. . . . Luckily, fish are plentiful; we have lobster on the daily menu. So it would be wrong to complain. Those on the continent have so much less than us, and have to deal with the bombs on top of that.

The war continues to rage on the mainland, as well as on the sea. One morning I go out with Albert and Jacques to do everything we can to recover the wrecks, which have just washed up on the islands. Albert sees a body floating a few meters from the shore. It is a German naval officer. We decided to take him back to the big island by towing him in my uncle's little dinghy, *La Chausiasie*. We leave him in the hold.

Our American friends come down to meet us, and we witness a surprising scene. Before anyone has time to do anything, one of them, a big man named Jack, noticing the German's gold dental work, takes out his pocketknife, loosens two or three teeth from the corpse, and puts them into his nostrils, all while laughing. It is a macabre and strange scene.[17]

PRISONERS

The Germans captured paratroopers and treated them ruthlessly. Normans witnessed these brutalities, which after four years of German rule did not really surprise them. Christian Letourneur remembers his encounter with the *paras* in this way:

The first paratroopers we saw were prisoners, watched over by German paratroopers recognizable by their round helmets. We were all in the kitchen when we heard a very loud knock on the door that led to the yard. It was a German officer, with around fifteen men who were guarding a group of unfamiliar soldiers without weapons or helmets. The soldiers had crewcuts and blackened faces. Their heads hung low and they looked exhausted. The German officer asked for *wasser*, and my mother gave him a pitcher of water and a cup. He seemed very nervous; as he drank, the top of the staircase leading to the bedrooms never left his gaze. After he had passed the water to his men, my mother tried to give a drink to the prisoners. She was brusquely pushed back, and the officer told her to go inside. As he closed the door, he said, "Don't be afraid!" and they disappeared into the yard. That was my first encounter with the paratroopers of the 101st Airborne.[18]

In Montebourg, north of Sainte-Mère-Église, Fernand Levoy looked out his window during the night of June 5–6, and saw the following:

> I noticed a group heading up the hill, with three guys in front dressed in khaki. We hadn't seen many soldiers in khaki; the Todt Organization were the only ones to dress that way. I said to myself, "That's not right! There is a German with a bayonet walking behind the Todt engineers!" Something was amiss. I ran to get my binoculars—I had a pair in my room—and when I looked, there was an American flag on the shoulder of the men I had taken for Todt engineers! Americans! All the locals had been expecting the English. I went down as quick as I could to tell Father Levoy.[19]

The Todt Organization was a Nazi military engineering group. Its major project in Normandy was the Atlantic Wall, a series of fortifications built along the northwestern shore of France in anticipation of an Allied invasion there. Toward the end of the war, every available German man was needed for combat, so the Todt Organization was composed of slave laborers, prisoners of war from conquered nations, and volunteers attracted by high wages.

When the curfew lifted at 6:30 a.m., Levoy went out to get a closer look at the prisoners.

> There were about a dozen prisoners, surrounded by a few Germans. The strong, athletic Americans' faces were painted black, and

they still had grenades around their necks. They gave us knowing winks, and V signs rose from their outstretched arms. The Germans stopped us from approaching the prisoners and told us it was forbidden to talk to them. We were able to get close to them anyway, and noticed that "Airborne" was written on one of their shoulders. Paratroopers![20]

Also from Montebourg, notary Eugene Legoupil learned how to communicate with the American prisoners without catching the attention of the Germans.

While the population is talking things over and getting organized, news of the landings spreads rapidly in the town. At first, information is very confused, peddled by the German troops or by civilians who say they are very well informed. According to them, the sea is covered with armored boats, torpedo boats, and big war boats. . . .

But what is the meaning of this gathering of civilians that forms suddenly near a truck on the place Jeanne-d'Arc, opposite the Kommandantur?[21]

It is the American paratroopers who have been picked up by the enemy from Sainte-Mère-Église. The soldiers guarding them point their machine guns on them. They seem to still be afraid of these giants with blackened faces who, before they were made prisoners, mercilessly fought a good number of their comrades. We learn that at Saint-Martin-d'Audoville, a group of paratroopers unexpectedly fell upon a platoon escorting French and foreign labor conscripts in the Todt Organization. Things went very quickly. Frozen with terror, the commanders loudly cried, "Comrade! Comrade!" but it made no difference to the Americans. They shot them point blank and threw the bodies in the ditch. At the first sight of their liberators, the workers, some hardly upset, dispersed into the countryside.

But for the moment, the American prisoners remain impassive. They jump from the truck, their guards at their heels, and are led to the guard post. There the "big caps" parade around and bark to see who can do it best. Before giving orders to his soldiers, an officer shouts in English, "Raise your arms!" All obey except one, the smallest of the group. He is wounded and holds his arm straight ahead. This brave boy—you can see him pinch his lips so as to hide his suffering.

We form a group of about twenty people up close to look at them. The Germans would so like to catch us in the act with a clumsy sign or word from the audience, but the conversations take place in low voices and as discreetly as possible.

The paratroopers are led away to the abbey, which has been transformed into a canteen. Other prisoners captured in the region subsequently come to join them, either in groups or individually. We see others now who seem more daring than the first ones. Hands on their helmets, they raise two fingers to form a V, all while smiling and looking at us. The Germans are not shrewd enough to catch it![22]

As Legoupil's story suggests, the Americans could also be brutal. Historians agree that the Normandy Campaign elicited viciousness from both sides. On the one side were the untested American soldiers, and on the other, the desperate German ones. Prisoners on both sides were on occasion shot without cause.[23] British paratroopers met a terrible fate as well. Irène Othon-Meillat remembers the Germans pitilessly shooting them down in Dozulé, east of Caen.

My name is Irène Othon-Meillat. In the period when the events took place which I am going to tell you about, I was living on a farm in the village of Dozulé. This fifth of June, 1944, I had decided to go visit friends who were living in Hérouvillette.[24] Around 11:00 p.m., there was a rumbling of planes flying low and scraping the roofs. At the same moment, the bombing started up again on the coast. You could hear the firing of automatic guns. . . . The gunfire grew increasingly loud; it seemed to be getting closer. We went back inside. After several hours, at around 2:00 a.m., everything once again became calm. It was too good to be true. With a friend we decided to go see what was happening. We didn't have the intention of going far, and actually we did not go far.

There were parachutes hanging in the trees. When we arrived at the top of the washing place, we found ourselves face to face with two completely blackened men. In the night you could see only the whites of their eyes. They had foliage on their helmets and were holding guns. One of them said to us, in near-perfect French: "Mesdames, don't be afraid. We are English. It's the landings; tell us where the Germans are." We knew that they were about two hundred meters away. I told them: "They are there, quite near." Then the Englishman said: "Leave quickly; you are going to get killed; go home." This is exactly what we did. But in going back, we saw that they were following us at a distance.

When we arrived at the house, there were already about twenty English paratroopers in front of the door, maybe more men of the Englishman who was following us. He caught up, and while unfolding his map, said to us: "We are looking for the shortest way for Ranville," adding that "we have been dropped too far." So we pointed out to them the direction to take in order to not be too close to the road. It was too dangerous.

At this moment, there is the sound of boots. "Get down and don't speak," he tells us. What a terrible fright! It turned out to be the [German] orderly of Captain Allemand. The latter was coming down from the chateau, where he was living, in order to rejoin his company, lodged in another castle a little farther away. I don't think he saw us, because we were back away a bit from the road. In any case, he continued on his way. By the time we were able to calm ourselves, no one was around. The paratroopers had disappeared. We went back into the house, and this time there was no question that we would stay there for the rest of the night.

Beginning on the morning of the sixth of June, around 5:00 a.m., the marine artillery pounded us for who knows how long. It was hell, a veritable deluge of fire. We all took refuge under a table at the farm. Our neighbor, whose husband was a prisoner of war, came to join us with her little six-year-old girl. We pressed against one another and prayed. That was about all we were able to do. . . . We were convinced that we were going to die.

Again on the morning of the sixth of June, 1944, we went out into the street and to the crossroads. We were stupefied to see a jeep arrive; we could not believe our eyes. At its side were four or five paratroopers standing. Everyone thought the Germans had left, including, I suppose, the paratroopers. But in fact they were still there. The Germans fired on the jeep, killing the paratroopers. Those who had not been killed they finished off with bare blows from the butt of their guns.

We thought we knew the horror of war, but there was much more in store for us. We went back into the house, and from the window on the second floor we could see the paratroopers descending. It was unbelievable. Gliders also landed, and the men crawled forward under their wings. The Germans fired on them; there were also battles with the bayonet. You also saw parachutes that did not open, and all those poor unfortunate men who crashed to earth. It was a horror.[25]

Sometimes Normans could rescue paratroopers from German imprisonment. Many of the German occupiers at that time were overage men convalescing from injuries received on the eastern front. Henri Manach, policeman at Caumont-l'Eventé, south of Bayeux, took advantage of these weaknesses in the German columns.

On the eleventh of June, in the middle of the afternoon, a farmer who lives on Saint-Lô road came to see us. "In the courtyard of my farm," [he said,] "I have 23 American soldiers, mildly or severely wounded, and guarded by some old German soldiers. The Germans asked me for something to drink. They are headed toward Cherbourg. I invited the leader into my house, and gave the guards and their prisoners something to drink. What should I do?" he asked us. Yes, what should we do? The Germans were old, with little fight in them. The situation was too tentative not to try to do something. "Okay, go home," we told him. "Give the Germans all that they want to drink. We will take care of the Americans at the opportune moment."

As I said, the Germans were not great fighters. For the most part, they could have been grandfathers. They let themselves drink too much and then some. We knew very well the effects of Calvados and hard cider. When the soldiers collapsed, we boarded the prisoners and brought them to the best possible shelter: the slate quarry.

They needed care. We told Dr. Picot about the situation, and he took his case, dressings, and medications and came to care for the wounded. He will actually care for them until the moment they are taken back by the American army. Bravo to him; he knew the risks that he was taking.

Who were these prisoners? We were able to get an explanation from them. They were part of the troops who landed in gliders in the region of Caen. All of them had been wounded and made prisoners at the moment of landing or soon afterward.[26]

A few days later, the village was liberated, and the twenty-three Americans rejoined the Allied forces.

BACK AND FORTH

Civilian safety was most precarious when a village teetered between Allied and German control. In these situations, liberation was at once close and yet far away. If Normans gave the Allies a cold welcome, it was usually because they feared reprisal should the Germans take their town again. Schoolteacher Marcelle Hamel-Hateau in Neuville-au-Plain, near Sainte-Mère-Église, experienced precisely this kind of switching back and forth between German and Allied control. Her story of June 6, begun in the previous chapter, continues in this way:

The dawn of the sixth of June begins to make the night grow pale. I shiver under the fresh breath of the morning hour. The Dumonts go away to their home, and we also go back to heat ourselves up a little in the warm, comforting ambiance of the house.

Suddenly, four or five soldiers with round helmets and guns in hand enter the courtyard. One of them, presumably the commander, knocks hard on the door while shouting, with a strong Yankee accent: "We are American soldiers. . . . Are there any Germans here?" His manner is so imperious and sure, you would think he had already won the war. We greet them with open arms. Their confidence is so contagious that we consider the Liberation to be already accomplished. As if the entire German army were obliterated in only one night! Moment of euphoria. I can no longer stand still. I go out, come back in, go, and come back through the entryway to the courtyard. I see paratroopers pass who, scraping the hedges, head toward their reassembly points. Most of them have a face that is smeared with black. They look at me, smiling drolly under their strange makeup. Several drag their legs; others are draped in the green and brown silk of their parachutes. Everything about them evokes the outlaws of the Wild West: their massive size and big round helmets, the large knife stuck inside the shaft of their beautiful, tall, yellow leather boots, their bearing and their gait. . . .

Another group of soldiers halts in front of the school and tries to orient itself. The officer makes a sign for me to approach. He is happy to notice that I understand English. He shows me on his map "La Chasse des Trois Ormes," on the edge of which is his rallying point. It's a small road just below, near the entrance to Sainte-

Mère-Église. Because the Americans want to avoid the main roads, the directions I provide are fairly complicated: you need to know the breaks in the hedges that allow you to cross them, and pass from field to field. I propose that I serve as their guide. Aware of the risks, the officer hesitates to accept my offer. But as he doesn't have any choice, he says "OK," all while chewing his gum and giving me a friendly tap on the shoulder. So we leave. As we are approaching Sainte-Mère, gunfire suddenly breaks out. The soldiers stop.

As for me, my heart was in my throat. If I were alone, I would have gotten myself out of there by running toward the house. But the Americans are there. There are still two fields to pass by running along the hedge. . . . I can see the road of Trois Ormes. Mission accomplished! Now I have to go the same route in the opposite direction and this time, alone. It seems as if it will never end. I have the sense that, as in a dream, I am marching in place without ever moving forward.[27]

When Madame Hamel-Hateau returns to her village, she is in for a huge disappointment.

Everyone in the village has now left their houses to greet the paratroopers, and the landings are already being celebrated; the Americans are invited to drink a shared bottle. Laughter, oohs! and ahhs! in response to all the new and astonishing things; for example, a bizarre little car, one of the first jeeps, which came down from the sky in a glider.

But our happiness does not last long. The Americans set up a small cannon at la Croix. It seems to me I hear the crackling of bullets. On the road I hazard down, a soldier is crouching behind the hedge. He remains still and bent over, as if on guard. As soon as he sees me, he mysteriously puts a finger to his lips, then points out something to me on the left. As soon as I turn my gaze in that direction, the words I am about to speak are strangled in my throat. At the bend in the road, German soldiers advance in single file with guns in hand, bending down, scraping the hedge. I realize the imminence of the danger and flee toward the house. No sooner do I get in than several rounds from machine guns make the windows shake. The Germans are still here! It's scarcely believable! ... In sum, by evening on the sixth of June, the situation, as we see it in Neuville, is not brilliant and is, in fact, very confused. We have not lost confidence, but the joy we felt in the morning has been replaced by a heavy anxiety.[28]

GRAIGNES

The most famous town alternating between American and German control was Graignes. About two hundred paratroopers, members of the 507th Regiment of the 82nd Airborne Division, landed there when they missed Amfreville, their drop point farther north. The Germans had flooded the River Merderet nearby; the area around the town had turned into swampland. Loaded down with equipment, many paratroopers perished as they landed in the swamps. Still others managed to cut themselves away from their chutes or were rescued by Normans in boats.

At first, the Germans were unaware that there were soldiers in Graignes, a village of nine hundred people. The Americans, led by Major Arthur Johnson, decided to stay there rather than fight their way north, back to their lines. Graignes was strategically located just south of Carentan. It was through this town that the Germans were retreating from the front while sending fresh units back up north. By keeping his soldiers in Graignes, Johnson sought both to harass the Germans from the rear and to cut off communication lines to southern regions.

Meanwhile, the mayor of Graignes coordinated relief efforts. The villagers provided food and first aid as well as intelligence concerning local terrain and German positions. Germaine Boursier, who ran the café, became the "mess sergeant" for the men, cooking food she had gathered by traveling throughout the region. Among those who rescued the men in the swamp was Denise Boursier-Lereculey.

We had seen them the same day, at three o'clock in the morning, but we could not yet really believe that they were our defenders. We were stuck on the idea that they were Germans disguised as Americans, and only afterward did we understand that the language was not the same. When they saw us, they cried out to us: "Bonjour, we are your friends, we have come to save you." As soon as possible, I went to warn my mother and my sister and invited [the men] to follow us, and gave them something to eat and good wine to drink. Then we made them a good fire, because the poor men were chilled to the bone and shivering; most of them had fallen into the water in their parachutes. But despite all this, they were afraid to enter, thinking that we were setting a trap. The same day, Major Johnson came to find us in order to ask us to please secure some supplies and food for these men. We accepted immediately. I then left the same night (the sixth) to warn the mayor to requisition the animals. Then I went in search of breakfast. The first two days, we had 170 men to feed, and the third day, it was 180 with the Russian, Mongolian, and Spanish prisoners, plus a Yugoslavian translator from Cherbourg. In addition, the major sent us two soldiers so we would not wear ourselves out. All of them were charming and impeccably correct in their dealings with the population; they were also greeted with joy and overwhelmed with gifts of meat, bread, butter, vegetables, stocks of fish, fruit, and wine by all the inhabitants of the surrounding communes.[29]

Madame S. Pezerin also remembers the rescue of the American paratroopers.

It was during the night of the fifth to sixth of June that the parachutists came down onto the territory of the commune of Graignes. The
morning of the sixth, after being frightened all night by the sounds
of planes and explosions, I am awakened by my teaching colleague.
She tells me to go down into the school courtyard, which is full of
soldiers with blackened faces who are literally falling asleep. They
ask each other a series of questions in English: Where are we? Are
there any Germans nearby? etc. . . . In all the trees and on the roofs
hung parachutes in every color. It is extraordinary. We make them
come in, and serve them coffee, that is, we warm up water so that
they can use it to dilute the soluble coffee and milk they have in
their rations. In order to inform them of the location of the Germans, I take my bicycle and leave for Tribehou, the neighboring
commune about six kilometers away. On the way I meet two Germans in a sidecar. They do not stop me. In Tribehou, I learn that
there are many of them [in the region]. On the way back, I think
perhaps [the two Germans] have gone up to Graignes, but I meet
them again. They have not dared to venture into the town. Tracks
left by their machines suggest they did a turnaround in the road.
This is a comfort.

Soon, groups of paratroopers arrive from all directions. We
greet them with open arms in our homes. Those who have fallen
in the swamp shiver and their teeth chatter. In all the houses, we
light large wood fires and give them warm drinks. The peasants
take out some old Calvados, which they had saved for this day since
the beginning of the occupation. The soldiers get acquainted with
the local liquor. We offer them something to eat and treat them like
old friends. As for them, they take marvelous things out of their
sacks—chocolate, cakes, matches fixed in a little carton, chewing gum, cigarettes. We exchange our old five-franc bills with the
new ones they show us—blue rectangles striped with green and a
bundle of French flags on the back side. Everyone shows photo-
graphs of their families. A very young father, who is wearing a ro-

sary around his neck, kept forcing us to admire the portrait of his wife and his adorable little girl. Still others reminisced about the "girlfriends" they had left behind two years ago in distant America. They are younger than they seem: fatigue no doubt ages them. They appear to be solid, well-built, and agile fellows. The entire population would do anything to please them, but they are so exhausted that they don't want anything else but to sleep. They fall down as one on the cement and sleep there for hours.

When they are all reassembled from every corner of the commune, a small troop forms under the command of the "major." General headquarters is established in the boys' school. The small school will be the infirmary and the operations room. While they get settled, we go up to the attic of the school. It is windy, and the sky is very gray. The sun is not shining enough to illuminate the extravaganza of colors due to the parachutes abandoned everywhere by their former owners. The soldiers give them as gifts to the families who greet them. . . .

All the men seem to be tired and hungry. Several were wounded in their jumps: some have cuts on their hands from using knives to cut their parachute lines and free themselves. Others are limping, but shots of novocaine instantly relieve their pain. They are wearing sturdy high boots that cover their legs and ankles. . . .

After the first hours of euphoria, a question surfaces: if the Germans attack, what will we do?

During the first two days, the paratroopers dug individual holes in the garden of the school and the surrounding fields. They camouflaged their radio equipment in the vegetable garden. They are without news of their comrades dropped on Amfreville. To keep the Allies from bombing the commune, large, pink phosphorescent signs were extended on the lawns in front of the school buildings. The planes flew low, making signals of friendship. But one evening, we are troubled by a plane with a swastika that grazes the town; we begin to fear bombs. Little by little, we settle into a new life.

To nourish the men, the peasants provide butter, milk, and calves, which the butcher slaughters. Someone is commandeered to do the cooking. The soldiers have a large coffee room at their disposal to have their meals. Everyone comes together to assure supplies for the troops despite the difficulties of the hour. Some risk their lives to go find flour at the mill in Airel, fifteen kilometers away . . . but they are stopped by a battle.[30]

Unfortunately, the joy and peace at Graignes would not last long. On Saturday, June 10, Major Johnson and his men succeeded in blowing up a major bridge outside of town in order to prevent the Germans from reaching Carentan. In the process, the Americans killed some Germans, so the enemy became aware of the *paras'* presence. The next day, Sunday, patrols initially concluded that the military situation remained quiet. The major allowed his men to attend Mass performed by the sixty-four-year-old priest Father Leblastier and his younger colleague, Father Lebarbenchon. In the middle of the service, a woman from the town burst into the church to alert the Americans that a sizable German infantry force was on its way. It turned out to be the 17th SS Panzer Grenadier Division, Götz von Berlichingen. The Americans rushed outside to defend the town, but did not allow the civilians to leave the church. Father Leblastier continued the service by reading *The Appearance of Fatima*, a book condemning World War I as God's punishment for sin.

The battle lasted most of the day, until the Germans retreated to get more ammunition. At this point, the Americans allowed members of the congregation to leave the church. The priests as well as several nurses stayed behind to tend to the wounded. Madame Pezerin remembers the events of June 11 in this way:

Every day and night, patrols explore the distant countryside. The Germans are not yet looking for a confrontation. Finally, on Thursday, the eighth of June, we begin to have alerts. There are no sirens to warn us, only very soft whistles that can be heard in the immediate area, that is, by us teachers continuing to live at the school as well as nearby shopkeepers. The Germans retreat to Carentan and pass on the road from the Port des Planques to Semnard three hundred meters from us. The Mongolians conscripted by the Germans give themselves up.[31]

For civilians in the surrounding region, Graignes has become a kind of tourist site. All the young people want to see the paratroopers, so much so that from morning until evening at the school there is a line of visitors bringing food and supplies. With his sweetness and gentleness, the "major," Abraham Sophian, wins all hearts. He serves as a translator for the young twenty-five-year-old commander, Arthur Johnson. The young Canadian Sergeant Boussard (who will be killed in the subsequent battles) surprises us with his French, which is so similar to the way the peasants speak. He remained legendary among us. All of them were eager to enter into action. So they began to "tease" the [German] armies that were scattered and falling back.

On Saturday, the tenth of June, at noon, the Americans blow up the bridge at the Port des Planques in order to cut off the German retreat route. That evening, you can sense a great deal of nervousness among both the officers and the men. . . . Sunday, the eleventh of June, dawns a radiant, glorious day. It is the feast of the Saint Sacrament, and the church bells are ringing out, muffling the distant noise of the cannon. We do not want to make ourselves conspicuous . . . but the threat is still there. The nest of paratroopers that we have sheltered with so much enthusiasm for five days now is going to cause our first wound.

Around 10:30 a.m., the alert is given. The faithful are already in the church when the battle begins. On the order of the captain, no one should leave before everything is over. . . . During these seemingly interminable hours, one hears the whistling of bullets and the bursting of mortars, which are responding to the clamor caused by the German bombs. Infernal and unforgettable sounds. While four of us were hiding under the table in the kitchen on the first floor, the school is hit in several places. The parts of the school at the rear of the building remain intact. Around 10:00 p.m., a rocket lights up the town; the cannon is silent. The battle is over . . .[32]

Here is how civilian Michel Folliot remembers that Sunday in Graignes:

Father Leblastier was celebrating Mass. The church was full. All the regular parishioners were there, as well as numerous civilians who never usually go to Mass. This was the case for the brother of my wife. Considering the danger, it is difficult to say if he was there out of devotion or curiosity. No doubt curiosity for many people, because a large number of the paratroopers were also going to Mass. Many of the Americans took Communion. As was the case every Sunday, there was a chorus and six musicians. As for me, I was playing the trombone. The Mass was progressing as usual.

There is no bakery in Graignes. Madame Barn had gone to get her bread in Tribehou.[33] On her way back, she noticed a German column headed toward Graignes. She hurried to the church to alert everyone. All the Americans present left in a hurry, and made the civilians stay in the church. Mass was almost over.

We were cloistered in the church while the battle began to rage outside. The music stopped dead and was replaced by dozens of people saying the rosary. Some of us went up to the clock tower to see what was going on. The battle lasted a very long time, and then finally, at the end of the afternoon, silence again reigned. Sergeant Boussard, who spoke French very well, went back into the church and told those persons who lived in the south of the commune to go home; the Germans occupied the north. It goes without saying that everyone said they lived in the south, including myself, and we left toward the houses in the south of the commune. I had taken the precaution of putting my trombone back into its box, and I took it with me. The Americans stopped me; they were suspicious that I was carrying weapons in this strange case.[34]

The battle began again about 10:00 p.m. Sunday evening and lasted until about 3:00 or 4:00 a.m. Monday morning. In that round, the church steeple, which now held two American snipers, was one of the first German targets. When both men refused to abandon their post, they were killed by the first round of German artillery. The outnumbered American troops soon ran out of ammunition. By the end of the battle, all but a handful had been killed. The Germans captured the church, which had been set up as an aid station and contained about twenty wounded soldiers. All twenty were likely murdered, either in the church, in a nearby field, or some days later in Le Mesnil Angot. The citizens of Graignes were also punished for their insubordination. Fathers Leblastier and Lebarbanchon were both murdered in the rectory along with their two housekeepers. The Germans then demanded that the villagers load the American dead into vehicles. Once again, Madame Pezerin takes up the story.

A group of SS bursts in on us at the kitchen door, where we are standing: three women and a child. After a summary examination of the place by the light of an electric lamp, they demand some wine. . . . But in Normandy after four years of occupation, we only have cider. They are very thirsty. But before quenching their thirst, they make one of us drink before them. Then they want to visit the house to find out if we are still hiding any paratroopers. They take one of us to accompany them upstairs and to the garden, forcing her to move forward with a revolver in her back! We are more dead than alive with fear, because we know that paratroopers occupy the attic. . . . The parachutes remain on the floor, but the men have jumped out the window.

Satisfied with their visit, they send us up to bed. Two of the bedrooms are demolished. The beds are strewn with glass. The armoire is resting on the bed, crossed by a bomb that did not go off. Two of our companions are exhausted and go to sleep, but we stay awake, meditating on the probable fates awaiting us. We expect to be shot as early as the morning. We ask ourselves what has become of the habitants of the four other houses in the town. Finally, the day breaks; the twelfth of June is here, but will we see its twilight?

In haste, believing that we could escape the surveillance of the guards patrolling us, we get ready to leave. We go no farther than the threshold of the door. With brutality, an SS officer makes us go back in. We get a glimpse of the church, which has been hit. The school presents a sad sight with its broken windows, its hanging drainpipes, its hole in the roof, and its windows enlarged due to missiles, their shutters torn away. We ask ourselves by what miracle have we escaped this flood of iron and fire. What has become of the wounded paratroopers we saw the evening before as they were transported from the school to the church? On the steps to the cemetery I saw traces of blood, with an American helmet resting nearby.

Our kitchen became the prison. We were unable to go out, and the habitants who passed through the town were brought to us. The machine gun is set up in the middle of the courtyard; we tell each other that we are going to be shot. The soldiers have brought in the trucks and are looting the houses and the grocery store. They make fun of us, come over to break the necks of the bottles in front of us while crying out with joy, greedily swallowing the cake they find, and loading blankets, dishes, even children's dolls and toys onto their vehicles.

Suddenly, we hear the low rumble of the little truck used by the farmers to carry their cans of milk. We hurry to the window to see the Germans bringing back the wounded paratroopers as well as some able-bodied prisoners. In front of us, they line them up along the wall of the "perelle" in a field facing the school, with their hands behind their heads. One wounded American, whose arm was bleeding, nevertheless also had to keep his hands behind his neck. All the while, the Germans are drunk, crazy, yelling loudly, "Invasion! . . . Invasion!"

At around 8:00 a.m., a German lieutenant arrives. He seems well rested and asks us what we are doing there. He allows us to leave. We go through the town running, because one of his companions who presided over the looting reproaches him for letting us leave. We are afraid he will change his mind. On our way, we come across several corpses: an American is lying in the entryway to a field; near a well, another is stretched out, arms crossed, face to the sky. The first house has been burned. Flat on our chests under the table of our kitchen, we were not able to imagine such a huge disaster. We head across the small fields toward the farm of Thieuville, which has been spared.

It was only the next day that we learned about the most tragic episode of that evening.

On the twelfth of June in the early morning, the wife of the sacristan goes, as she does every day, to bring the milk for the parish priest's lunch. At the door of the presbytery she meets the Germans, who tell her: "Pastor left." But as she has noticed two little pools of blood, she enters with her husband and finds the bodies of the two priests covered with sticks, riddled with bullets, the skulls shattered. Father Louis de Gonzague has a bullet in the eye; his glasses are on the ground. The face of Father Leblastier bears the marks of a great suffering. Both have been robbed of their watches and the money they were carrying. Father's suitcase is open and almost empty. The mayors of Graignes and of Mesnil Angot, assisted by some municipal counselors and the housekeeper, who had left the presbytery the evening before, wash the bodies of the two martyrs, and dress them in priestly robes. They show them in the great room with the intention of burying them together. Although access to the town was forbidden to all civilians, even to gravediggers, they are able to place the bodies in coffins on Sunday the twenty-fifth. But when Tuesday the twenty-seventh arrives—the day on which they were to be buried—the enemies set fire to the presbytery. The bodies, taken out of the coffins, rest on the floor and are burned.

Neither did the Germans want us to pay our last respects to the paratroopers who fell in a courtyard next to the presbytery, where they were violently thrown into a drinking trough. One of them had a bayonet still thrust in his back.

But what became of the other paratroopers? Only a few corpses are found. We saw a dozen prisoners the day after the battle. We hope that they have been able to flee. They were living in the commune for a week and became familiar with all the little paths. Some have taken boats belonging to the fishermen of the Saint Pierre port. In this way, sixty-three passed under the noses of the Germans to go find the American troops in Carentan. For twenty-four hours, the inhabitants fed them and hid them in attics under the hay. A worrisome detail: one had been forced to take a bath, and had a terrible cough. How then to keep him quiet when the German patrols crisscrossed the villages?[35]

The Germans commanded the inhabitants of Graignes to leave. Those who argued were shot on the spot. American soldiers continued to hide in the area for several days, and some were able to fight or sneak their way back to the American lines with the help of civilians. One of these was Madame Odile Delacotte.

We were four families who had been evacuated from the region stretching from Cherbourg to Graignes, near Carentan. We had eighteen-month-old babies, and we could not stay in Cherbourg. (We were called "refugees.") We were living in a large house in Graignes. . . . At dawn on the sixth of June, we heard the sound of feet in boots, voices in the courtyard, and violent knocks on the door. We opened it and saw a dozen American soldiers. With guns in hand, they came into the room. They were wet, having fallen into the swamp. They made a sign for us to line up along the wall, with the two eighteen-month-old babies in our arms, while they cleaned their wet guns on the big table. Then they took out a map of the Manche and showed us a point: Sainte-Mère-Église.

We showed them Graignes on the map, and they appeared to be worried. The young girl, Yvette, spoke a little English, and they explained to her that they were supposed to have landed in Sainte-Mère-Église, but because of an error, they landed in Graignes. (Another version was that German anti-aircraft fire had hit the plane, forcing them to be released in Graignes above the swamp.) There were about fifty soldiers in the village, and when they saw that there were no Germans in town, they became reassured and friendly. For eight days, we became American, and everyone in the village brought them butter, meat, and fruit, and we were all happy, but alas, it did not last!

The following Sunday, we were at Mass in the church, along with a group of American soldiers, some of whom kept guard around the church. Suddenly, a soldier entered and cried, "The Germans are coming!" The American soldiers left and prepared for battle, and as for us, we knew to get home and close ourselves in. All day long and into the evening, they fought in and around the church until they ran out of ammunition, because the Americans did not have a great deal.

The morning brought peace once again, but the German soldiers stayed in the village and inhabited the houses. We had six of them in our house, and we had to live with them. They were nice enough and were in the Wehrmacht. One of them, an Alsatian, spoke French. What had become of our parachutists and the other American soldiers? No one knew, but certainly several of them had been killed. But there was nothing we could do about it. . . .

One morning, Yvette and I went to bring food to the rabbits, who were in a cowshed under the hayloft a little distance away. We heard noise and the rustling of pines, and then we saw the heads of two visibly thinner men, who were looking at us and making a gesture to be quiet. It was two of the paratroopers. Yvette spoke with them and asked them what they wanted to eat; they asked for sugar and milk, because they had eaten nothing for several days except hearts of cabbage! We then realized that the animal we had accused of eating the hearts of cabbage was, in fact, two Americans who ventured out every night.[36]

DEVASTATION

For the Normans, liberation was at best bittersweet. Some nineteen thousand were killed. Hundreds of thousands more lost their homes and possessions. Such towns as Le Havre, Caen, and Saint-Lô became "martyred" towns, almost completely wiped off the map. "Every family had lost someone," remembered American journalist Andy Rooney. "It was true that they were being freed but at the cost of the total destruction of everything they had."[1]

Most deaths occurred as a result of bombing. The Allies dropped 550,000 tons of bombs onto France in the years 1942–44. In the months before the Norman Invasion, Allied planes attempted to destroy the nation's transportation system as well as its armament industry. In the process, they also demolished thousands of farms and homes. The Nazis used the devastation as a propaganda tool, claiming that Great Britain and the United States had imperial aims in France. In this way, the Germans hoped to turn the population against the Allies. To some extent, they succeeded in doing so.

But nothing could compare to the scale of destruction Normans endured in the first twelve days after the landings, when over seven thousand civilians perished from bombing raids. With little help from the Germans, civilians were forced to survive on their own as best they could. No place was safe, and escaping death became largely a matter of luck.

BETWEEN TWO ENEMIES

On Monday evening, June 5, Allied bombers made their way to the French coast to destroy German artillery batteries in the region. Because of bad weather and imprecision in reaching targets, some batteries went untouched, while many civilians were killed. At dawn on June 6, American bombers unloaded still more deadly cargo on coastal towns, this time to prevent Nazi troops from rushing toward the beaches. Those directly subjected to the bombardments along the Cotentin coast sought shelter in trenches outside their homes. Some of these were communal, some private. Some had been constructed by civilians, others built then abandoned by Germans.

Despite these shelters, the night of June 5–6 brought fear, destruction, and death. Marcel Destors, his wife, and his family were among the unlucky Normans whose town had been bombed that night. Marcel was a prosperous farmer and a chief in the local Passive Defense. In the absence of German guidance, community leaders had organized their own response systems for wartime emergencies. Men like Marcel were to coordinate rescue and medical efforts in case of a bombardment.

The Destorses lived in the coastal town of Maisy, at the base of the Cotentin Pensinsula and between the two beaches—code-named Omaha and Utah—used for the American landings. Hence the Destorses found themselves in the middle of the invasion on the morning of June 6. Here is how the events of the day unfurled for them, as recorded by Madame Destors in her personal diary:

> June 5, 3:15 a.m. I am awakened by the sound of airplanes turning and scraping the roofs. Then there is a strong explosion. To see, I go to the window in the boys' room, which is open. A large red column of smoke rises up from les Perruques.[2] "It looks like les Perruques has been hit again," Marcel says as he comes to join me. In their pa-

jamas, the boys also come to see. Yves, who is eighteen months, begins to cry. I go to him and hold him in my arms, kneeling by the
cradle. He calms down as I talk to him and embrace him.

The bombs fall in bursts with a frightful noise; it's a rain of fire.
We thought it was coming from behind the house, but in fact it's
coming from the other side, very near to us! The windows explode,
the floor trembles like a tree shaken by a storm; the dust falls everywhere, and an odor of gunpowder tugs at our throats. Kneeling near the cradle, I pray with all my soul! "Be so good, my Lord,
to bless our house with your presence tonight!" At this moment
Marcel, who had gone up to look for the little ones upstairs, comes
down with them. They are in their pajamas with their feet bare,
paying no mind to the fact that they are walking on broken glass.

"Quick, to the trench," says Marcel . . . I am seized with fear at
the prospect of going out in this dreadful, deadly storm, but I put
on a flannel bathrobe and wrap the baby in it. I find my slippers
by the light of the bombs. Brigitte carries Dominique, who is still
sleeping. The prodigious sleep of childhood! The boys follow in silence. Downstairs in the dining room, broken glass covers the floor.
The little ones pass me my fur-lined coat and put on their own coats
over their shoulders. Then we are outside, running with our precious burden until we reach the back of the garden. We can see it
clearly despite the dark. The air stinks of gunpowder.

Finally, we slip into our trench. The trip across the garden
seemed to last forever. It is raining softly. The earth is so dry that it
immediately absorbs the rain. A new burst of fire crashes down on
us, tearing the air apart and making the earth shake! We hold on to
one another tighter and tighter in order to make ourselves smaller!

"I'm going to see what's become of the servants!"says Marcel. A
few minutes later, he arrives with Elizabeth and Auguste. He brings
the big umbrella to shelter us from the rain. The planes still fly
overhead, but no more bombs fall. The air clears a bit. Marcel soon

leaves again, this time for the town. "I'm going to see what's become of them down there . . . Don't wait for me. Go back in when the airplanes become far away."

The bombardment lasted a half hour. Toward 4:00 a.m., we go back inside, look for matches, candles, and shoes because, apart from me, everyone has bare feet. The dining room is no longer anything more than a pile of tiles on the courtyard. In the corridor, one window is opened, a second has a torn lower bar; a third has survived. Huge pieces of glass litter the floor. In my bedroom, panes have fallen behind the shutters and protrude into the courtyard.

We go to bed again after a fervent prayer of thanks. I am not able to go to sleep, and I worry about the town and the prolonged absence of Marcel.

Finally, he returns at 6:00 a.m.!

"It's a disaster," he tells me, "the entire center of the town is wiped out! The Sehier family is under the rubble, as are Mauret's wife and their son, as well as the entire Clément family! . . . Give me some sheets so I can bury their bodies. I just brought two to the city hall. Mauret's wife is in pieces, disemboweled. It's horrible!"

Thanks to God for having protected us.

We embraced each other, overwhelmed with emotion.

Marcel goes off again to his difficult task, as always courageous, thinking of others, demonstrating his qualities of leadership.

The young German soldiers camped near us come to wash at the pump, as they do each morning. A stick of bombs hit them at ten meters' distance, so they are distraught. The children wake up, one after the other; I let them sleep. Their appetite is minimal.[3]

Like the Destorses, Fernand Broekx woke up to find himself in the thick of things in Colleville-sur-Mer, directly south of Omaha Beach. He could hear the bombing of Maisy several miles west. Then the bombs reached him. Broekx's account also demonstrates how Normans sometimes had to deal with increasingly desperate German soldiers.

On the sixth of June around two o'clock in the morning, the bombing began, as it had in previous days, along the coast of Maisy. We were not too alarmed. After I got up, I went back to bed, but I was not able to get back to sleep. Around four in the morning, the noise seemed to get closer, so I got up again and shuttled back and forth between my bedroom and the courtyard. Around 6:00 a.m., the situation seemed to me to be worrisome. I went upstairs again to tell my wife: "I think it's time you got up." At this time, I will honestly confess that I was afraid. I had the feeling that the house was going to collapse on us. The walls were damaged and the floorboards lifting up. You could hear the tiles falling, one after the other, as well as the crash of breaking glass. The volleys of naval cannon and the bombs released by planes made a deafening racket.

The coast was nothing more than a gush of flames. Soon a cloud of black smoke rose up more than two thousand meters high: hard to believe it was the middle of the night. A strong odor of powder caught at our throats. We went downstairs, and I said to my wife: "Let's place ourselves at the entryway on the side opposite the sea. That's the best way to shelter ourselves from the bombs coming from the sea." I went upstairs to my room once more to look for some things I had forgotten. Soon afterward, an exploding bomb broke the kitchen window and struck the wall at an angle. It ricocheted against a partition, and literally turned around my wife, who was hit by a small fragment. She went across the street to our neighbors, where I found her and noticed that her wound was not serious.

Under the fire of the bombardment, I did not hesitate to come back home where, calmly, I turned on the stove to heat up a cup of real coffee, which we had painstakingly saved for the day when we would need a tonic. This beverage was greatly appreciated by our neighbors. A typical detail: as we no longer had bread, I set about making crepes. We took refuge across the street at our neighbors' house, which seemed more solid than our own.

In the afternoon, the Germans came to ask me for something to eat, but believe me, I refused to give them whatever I had. Around eight o'clock in the evening, two other Germans approached my house. Because they acted as if they wanted go in, I went and stood in front of them, then asked them what they wanted. One of them responded with these words: "We want blankets." I told him: "I don't have any." He made a show of anger. Without hesitation, I took him roughly by the arm and led him to the entry of our cellar while telling him: "Here we are twenty-three in number. There are women and children among us, including a mother with a two-month-old baby on her arm." They didn't look convinced. Ultimately, we gave them a very light bedcover as well as a sack, just to have some peace. About twenty minutes after this little confabulation, our unwanted guests threw a torpedo in our direction, but it fell twenty meters beyond us onto a farm, setting it on fire. We were unable to do anything to confine the fire, because machine guns constantly fired from our side. . . .

On the seventh of June around four or five o'clock in the morning, the majority of the Germans seemed absolutely exhausted. In general, they were young men of sixteen to eighteen years. . . . To an officer who spoke French, I said: "What are you waiting for in order to surrender? You no longer have anything to keep fighting." With a desolate air he responded: "What can you do? These are our orders." . . . Finally, at noon on the seventh, we heard tanks going by on the road from Port-en-Bessin to Grandcamp. I rushed over to the road, and there I saw my first Americans appear. The thought that we were finally delivered from an oppression which had lasted four years made our enthusiasm border on delirium.[4]

CAEN, MARTYRED CITY

The most destructive raids were still to come. In order to stop German troops from rushing northward into the peninsula, Allied planners sought to destroy the transport arteries of Norman cities, including Caen, Lisieux, Condé-sur-Noireau, Argentan, Saint-Lô, Vire, and Coutances. To do so, they argued, the centers of these towns had to be decimated by bombing, their ruins transformed into choke points. Allied commanders vigorously debated this plan. To target cities with large civilian populations, historic sites, and absolutely no military installations was deemed unacceptable by many of them.[5]

In the end, the argument for necessity won the day. The Allies issued warning leaflets dropped from planes. Civilians were urged to evacuate cities as soon as possible and find refuge in the countryside. Unfortunately, however, wind and weather scattered most of these fragile missives.[6] Many inhabitants simply did not realize the danger they were in. On the evening of June 6, the targeted cities were bombed first by the Americans, then by the British. By dawn the next day, entire cities had ceased to exist, and thousands of Normans were dead.

Here is how fifteen-year-old Danièle Philippe remembered the bombing of Caen on D-Day. In her diary dated June 6, she wrote the following:

All of a sudden, someone yelled out, "Planes are diving! Quick, everyone inside!" We had enough time to catch a glimpse of the planes. They had a white star on the fuselage and a strange tail with two rudders shaped like plates, which were connected to the elevator. The planes flew at low altitude, and there was a strident whistling noise as they passed over our heads. But they didn't shoot!

We rushed into the trench. Phew! It couldn't have come sooner!

We had barely gotten to safety when all hell broke loose. Terrorized little children began to scream as the machine guns tore up the area above us. The planes returned to attack, one after another. They swooped down on us and fired continuously. One woman was screaming as the children around her sobbed. I wondered when the infernal racket would finally end. It was the lowest the planes had ever flown! We had the horrifying impression that they were targeting us, that we already had one foot in the grave and our only option was to sit and wait. What did they all want from us? I wanted to rise up in revolt—against whom, I did not know. I felt like crying out: "This is your 'great' liberation? We are all meant to get our share? Our world was calm before you arrived. Perhaps it wasn't terrific, but at least we had a chance to make it out in one piece, whereas now . . ." The din was enough to drive one mad. If only the kids would stop their wailing! And their mother! Mercy!

"She should shut her mouth!" yelled Colette, who had limited herself to plaintive sighs up until that point. I was relieved that my sister was brave enough to bring the woman into line. You have to pull yourself together!

It was hard to believe, but we didn't hear any more noise outside. We listened closely. Silence, at last! It was over! Everyone in the trench calmed down as well. Someone next to us abruptly started laughing uncontrollably. It was a strange, wild guffaw. We were all on edge . . . but alive! We survived!⁷

Caen exemplified the martyred towns of D-Day. The city was a key transportation center as well as a hub for armor and plane production. Bombing on the night of June 5 had failed to destroy the bridges across the Orne, the city's main river. These missed targets led to further raids the next day. As the first of these attacks began at 1:30 p.m., the Caennais were sitting down to lunch. For hundreds of them, it would be their last meal. Young Jacqueline Sabine remembers that *déjeuner* in Caen vividly.

After a rather austere breakfast, Mother hesitated as she decided whether or not to do the washing—the laundry had been soaking in the sink since the night before. She took off her watch and began to rub the washboard with the old brown soap, and also found the time to prepare the midday meal with rutabagas, our ever-present companion.

Once the house was tidy, at 12:30–1:00 p.m., we sat down for lunch. After we finished eating and cleared the table, we suddenly heard the roar of bombers. My father went to the window and yelled, "Twin tails are dropping leaflets on the town!"

Leaflets had, in fact, been dropped hours earlier—we saw them later—but when the second wave of planes arrived, a violent impact shook the house, and all three of us hunkered down in the corner of the room. My father turned over the large wooden table for use as a shield. The noise of everything rattling was terrifying. When it was all over, we found ourselves in the dark. There was an opaque cloud of dust outside, shattered glass all over, and the hallway transom had been displaced. We heard screaming and wailing. "Everything behind us toward rue St. Jean has been flattened, and there is a fire," Papa said. "Your mother and I are going to go down and see if we can help attend to the wounded with the emergency teams."

A few months prior, I had had my kidney removed due to tuberculosis, and I was still convalescent and fragile. The surgeon said to my parents, "It will be five years before she gets her full energy back."

I was sad not to be able to help the victims, and well aware of how dangerous it was to stay on the fourth floor of an old house with a shaky foundation. So I packed a small suitcase with clean underwear, a pair of pants, two skirts, and some sweaters, and grabbed the little cash left in the house as well as some jewelry (but I forgot the watch next to the sink!). I added a small packet of photos and closed up the bag.

When my parents got back, they were devastated from what they had seen, the wounded and the damage done. I persuaded them to leave town by bike: "They'll surely come back, because they're trying to hit the commandant." After a look back at our family home of twenty years, filled with the warmth created by love and my parents' hard work, I said a final goodbye. For I knew deep inside that I would never again see my books, college notes, my freshly typed diploma, the beautiful print of the Louvre pinned to the wall in my little study corner; the pretty crystal vase that Raymond gave to me on Labor Day; all my letters of love and friendship—the treasures of my youth![8]

When she returned to her home some weeks later, Jacqueline found it obliterated. On the night of June 6, bombs had again fallen from the sky in Caen, this time in order to block the advance of the German 12th and 21st Panzer Divisions. Fires had consumed what bombs did not destroy. Also an adolescent in 1944, Jacques Perret describes the terror of that night. Like thousands of others, he wondered why the city was being bombed.

We were used to being awakened in the middle of the night by the air raid sirens, and would listen carefully to hear whether the sound of the Flying Fortresses or the sharp, metallic sound of anti-aircraft fire was drawing closer or becoming more distant.

The recent bombing of Caen was, alas, fresh in our young minds. We knew that the rising whirr of the engines meant that the planes had just dropped their deadly load. It was a terrifying thought. Who was the target?

On that night, the fracas in the skies was akin to a powerful storm that refused to leave the coast. We children were all huddled in the same bedroom to give one another strength, while our parents came in and out, trying to calm us down.

Our eldest sister, Marie-Madeleine ("Mamad" for short), was

eighteen at the time. She was suffering from a pulmonary illness and was very distressed by what was happening. Her injury in 1943 had put her through a tremendous ordeal. The sirens and planes would make her completely lose control of her senses. She would become completely motionless. After that night, my father decided to dig a trench far away from the house, at the edge of the yard. He clearly did so just to put his mind at ease, because we barely used it. The sirens increasingly went off during the night and would be followed by a "light show." This terrified us so much inside the house that no one particularly wanted to see what was going on outside.[9]

Once the bombs detonated, the lives of injured civilians depended on local hospitals. With little medical and ambulance support available, many who could have been saved instead perished. First-aid stations were subject to the destructive effects of bombing, so they were set up in sheltered areas, such as basements and caves. Sometimes police stations, town halls, schools, or private homes had to do. Yvonne Mannevy, a thirty-eight-year-old nurse living in L'Aigle, southeast of Caen, provides vivid testimony concerning the city's medical difficulties when it was once again bombed on the afternoon of June 7.

All of a sudden, there was a horrendous bang, and we were struck by window glass. We immediately understood what was going on and took cover in the cellar with the housekeeper, who had just arrived. After the explosions had stopped, I was halfway down the stairs when I realized I had to leave for my aid station. So I went back upstairs to fetch my nurse's blouse and my armband on the first floor. Along the way, I had just enough time to catch a glimpse of the double door in the living room, which had been completely warped by the blast. I went onto the balcony in my mother's room, which overlooked the town. It was horrifying. Flames everywhere. The hospital was ablaze, as was the rue Porte Rabel, and the train station had been hit. In the foreground, I had a full view of the back of the rue Saint-Barthélémy and the rue des Jetées. The houses had been laid to waste. Particularly striking was the huge cloud of dust above L'Aigle. My mother followed me upstairs and yelled, "Where did it hit?" "Everywhere!"

At that very moment, more planes arrived. There were only a few minutes between the two waves. Mother didn't even have time to reach the balcony. We went back into the room. I finished getting dressed and left.

I entered town through the Saint-Barthélémy neighborhood to reach the town hall, where the Passive Defense people would be meeting. Everywhere I looked, there were caved-in houses, dead bodies on the ground, and people screaming. That same morning, those same people had been living peacefully in their houses; in the blink of an eye, the town had turned into a lunar landscape. At Quai Catel, I passed in front of the house of Dr. Frinault, the radiologist at the hospital. His wife was at the gate, concerned about her husband, whose whereabouts were unknown.

I was able to climb through the ruins to rue des Emangeards and Notre-Dame de Marie boarding school, which had effectively been transformed into a hospital. It was unbelievably chaotic in the courtyard: people laid out everywhere, new wounded arriving, parents picking up their children . . . Monsieur Gaston Beauchef and his son René, both surgeons, led the operations. They decided to set up there instead of at their clinic, which was too small and had suffered heavy damage, in any case. The elder Monsieur Beauchef sent me to the hospital to try to find boxes containing sterile surgical instruments.

I left for the hospital by way of rue de la Madeleine. It wasn't a pretty sight. I ran up it as best I could. The hospital was on fire. During the first wave, bombs had hit the chapel and the cloister.[10] The radiology department had been destroyed, and a nun and two nurses had been killed. Some had succeeded in leaving through the cloister, but there were quite a few wounded, and people were still trapped under the rubble. At the moment of the blast, Dr. Frinault had said, "We have to take cover in the surgery department, inside the elevator. We'll be safe there." For his part, Dr. Foisy had been in favor of staying in the glassed-in hallway that connected radiology to surgery, an area that wouldn't collapse under the rubble. There was a second barrage of bombs, and this time, surgery took a direct hit. The metal elevator car fell, and Dr. Frinault was literally cut in two. Meanwhile, Foisy and the others were covered in shards of glass and rendered deaf by the explosions, but they still had their lives. The surviving patients were out in the street, on the sidewalk, lying on mattresses or stretchers.

At the foot of a spiral staircase, I came across the ass that we would see every day, pulling the cart to the bakers' to get bread. It was dreadful. The poor beast had been disemboweled, its entrails had spilled out, and its eyes were bulging out of their sockets. It doesn't make sense; I had just seen heaps of dead human bodies, but this was the image that would remain etched in my memory.

I ended up finding a nun, who said she had been able to salvage several boxes of instruments. She had set them down in the corner of a nearby pasture. I took a wheelbarrow—they were heavy—and began the task of returning to town, which was quite difficult due to the condition of the roads and the debris that was obstructing them. In the end, it turned out that the instruments I had worked so hard to bring back were not the ones they needed.

Then night fell. I remember a comical scene. In the dorm for the youngest boarders, there was a man lying in a crib. It was far too small for him, to say the least—more than half of his legs were hanging off the end. He asked me to wipe his face. His arms were completely wrapped in bandages, and he was sweating profusely. It was Monsieur Martin, the notary on rue des Emangeards. He wasn't seriously injured—if you didn't count the many cuts on his hands and forearms—but very easily could have been. He had gone up to the attic and opened the skylight to see what was going on. His house was blown away by the second wave. He found himself where he had been, at the window of his attic room . . . but on the sidewalk. If it weren't for his curiosity, he would have been crushed under the rubble.

Madame Frinault came to join us as well. She had learned that her husband had died. But she was a vivacious woman and came to do her part, to keep her mind off the tragedy. She spent the night comforting people and calming the distressed. It was a beautiful thing.[11]

When Caen was finally liberated, only 25 percent of the town remained. Of the original sixty thousand inhabitants, a mere eight thousand still had homes to call their own.[12]

USING YOUR EARS

Unlike England or Germany, bomb shelters were rare in France. For the most part, the French were left to look out for themselves. They developed expert ears, learning how to estimate the altitude of bombers and to determine whether a bomb was whistling overhead or silently headed straight for them. Twenty-three-year-old seamstress Paulette Osouf lived with her family in Coutances, another city bombed several times on D-Day, most horribly that night. Even on June 6, Osouf had already cultivated a masterly sense of hearing, and could warn her family of the danger coming from above. Unfortunately, no one would listen to her.

The first fright came at 1:00 p.m., when three bombs landed in a field behind the train station. It was over so quickly that we didn't realize what had happened. There was no anti-aircraft fire. At our house, a little piece of shrapnel broke the attic window and lodged itself in the beaten earth floor. Our joy soon gave way to fear and anxiety. At around 6:00 p.m., more bombs landed behind the train station. It was more violent than before; we were very scared and on edge.

At 7:40 p.m., we set the table for a dinner of vegetable soup and sand eel, which would never be eaten. I was nervous and couldn't keep still, so I went out into the courtyard to listen. When I came back inside, I said: "I hear planes. They're high up, very high, but there are a lot of them, a whole lot. They're coming our way, we have to go." No one would listen. Mother got angry and said, "Please, just eat and leave us be." I pleaded from my seat near the window. If the window broke, it would fall on my head. I closed the window catch. "I hear planes coming in our direction," I insisted. "We have to go." They called me mad, crazy, and unhinged. My older sister said, "She thinks she's Joan of Arc. Joan of Arc heard voices, and she hears planes. It's sad, really."

But at 8:00 p.m., everyone heard the planes. My older sister rushed to the bedroom to get a statuette of the Immaculate Conception that she kept on the table.

Everyone left their seat and began saying the rosary. The first bombs fell immediately thereafter. We yelled out in fear, "They're bombing!" Papa tried to calm us by saying, "Don't worry, it's only machine gun fire." We knew otherwise. Then the second string of bombs fell. My younger sister grabbed ahold of Papa's arm and yelled, "I'm scared! I'm scared!" Papa had just enough time to reply, "There's nothing to be afraid of. As long as we don't hear whistling, they're not coming our way." And then we didn't hear a thing—it was finished, the third had our name on it. Three hundred and fifty Flying Fortresses bombed for twenty-five minutes, and we didn't hear anything.

It's impossible to accurately depict the state we were in. We hadn't fainted and we weren't sleeping, but we were unconscious. The feeling is indescribable; it's almost as if we were under anesthesia, in a deep sleep.

After a moment, I regained consciousness. I had been hit by falling debris and stones, especially on my feet. So I lifted my feet up, thinking to myself, "I don't want to be buried alive." My eyes were open but it was very dark, darker than the darkest of nights. That only lasted for two or three seconds, and then I lost consciousness again.

After quite a long time, I regained my senses. My sister writhed in my arms. I took her by the hair and told myself, "I'm not going to let go. Dead or alive, I'm going to get her out of here." And then I was again out of sorts. Incapable of speaking. But I wasn't afraid; it was dreamlike, unreal. I felt like I was the only one with a survival instinct.

We all snapped out of it at the same time, as if we had been awakened from a dream. It was still dark, but I saw a glimmer of daylight. I was the first to speak: "There's daylight." "There's daylight," echoed Papa, then a second, a third, and a fourth voice. I exited through what I thought was a small hole, but was actually the door frame (I couldn't see anything because of the thick plume of dust). Papa was next to go out, followed by the rest of the family. Papa counted us, and everyone was there. "Everyone OK?" "Yes." It was a miracle: we all had our two arms, our two legs, and our two eyes. Papa did have a large cut under one eye and on his head.

The surprising thing was how incredibly calm we were. My younger sister had lost her shoes. She calmly searched for them in the rubble. Another who had lost one shoe didn't even think to look for it and came out with one shoe on. I still had mine, because they were tied on at the ankles.

We were trapped in the little courtyard. Papa thought to use a ladder to climb over the neighbor's wall, but how could we find one amid all this clutter?

I turned around and saw a bit of daylight coming through the neighbor's house. "Maybe we can go through there." The opening, about fifty centimeters wide, was at the top of the window. We slipped outside, where we found ourselves on top of two meters of debris. We were stunned. We had thought that our house was the only one that had been hit, but there was absolutely nothing left around it. The whole neighborhood was in ruins. Panic and terror set in when we saw the train station and realized the magnitude of the disaster.

As a result of the bombing in Coutances, 312 civilians lost their lives. The town was 65% destroyed.

Normans created their own shelters. Medieval castles offered thick walls and were big enough to shelter entire villages. No one wanted to die alone. Claude Paris describes how his family in Saint-Lô survived the bombardments of the night of June 6–7.

> Planes were continuously flying overhead, and we heard the boom of mortar fire in the distance. The Germans who had fled the fighting at Omaha had come to regroup their lines of defense. Instinctively, the families tried to gather together by village. Solitude breeds fear. Many chose the cellar of the castle, which had 1.6-meter-thick walls—a place where at least you were sure to be safe.[13]

Sometimes survival meant having indifferent rather than acute ears. When the cows had to be milked, according to Paris, a woman who was hard of hearing stepped forward to do it. "One day when she was leaving, everyone tried to stop her, because the bombs were falling at a steady rate. Her response was: 'No bother, I don't hear a thing.'"[14]

PRAYERS AND MIRACLES

Excellent ears could help you know when and where the bombs were coming. But they could not stop them from falling. Normans often turned to prayer as their only recourse for survival. Marcelle Hamel-Hateau describes a bombing raid near Sainte-Mère-Église.

Whirrrr . . . Kaboom! Windows shatter. A shell had just hit very close to us. Not a German shell—it was the Americans striking back. Their little planes were flying back and forth, and every time we heard the "Whirrrr . . . Kaboom!" it was because they had located a German artillery position and dropped a bomb. Heaven help us!

I clung to my mother under the mattress and took her hand. My little dog, which was normally full of pep, huddled up with us and remained silent and motionless. The whirr of the shells picked up pace and grew nearer. The interval between the whistling noise and the explosion became shorter and shorter. Each time, we tucked in our shoulders and our muscles tightened, as if to protect ourselves from the blow.

Kabooom! A deafening explosion hit! I couldn't hear a thing! The shell landed so close that I didn't even hear it whistle. Once I'd snapped out of my initial shock, I ventured to the window to take a peek outside. Monsieur Dumont's house had disappeared behind a cloud of dust and smoke. There was a moment of silence; then I saw Monsieur Dumont and his three children run across the yard. They were pallid and trembling when they came inside. We crawled out from under our mattresses to welcome them in. A shell had just blown through their house.

Our little group was in a state of panic. Mother said prayers as a way of deflecting her fears. Grandmother had the kids pray, "God protect us! Lord, have pity on us!" As soon as she took a pause from the litany, I urged her to go on, because even though I'm hardly a believer, it was the best way to redirect the fear of the children and adults alike. "Saint Marguerite, patron of Neuville, protect us. O Mary conceived without sin." The Germans seemed panicked themselves. I could hear them talking, walking, and running. Some came into our house, walked through the hallway, and went up to the attic to take shots through the skylight. They didn't really see us, apart from a quick, slightly deranged glance as they passed by. They finally moved their gun once they knew they had been spotted. It was too late for us, unfortunately.

The window flew open with such a bang that the noise of shattered glass was a soft note amid the horrid clamor. The house cracked eerily, seemingly blown apart by the hellish cyclone of dust. The stench of gunpowder irritated our throats. I was beyond fear, in a trance. No feeling whatsoever. Completely out of sorts. I ceased to exist. I imagine that this is how someone who is killed instantly passes into the afterlife. My return to consciousness was lukewarm and wet, in the form of a lick on the nose from my little dog.

It was impossible for us to immediately gauge the full scale of the damage. We stayed under our mattresses—the gun battle had resumed with even greater intensity. In the evening, when it calmed down and we began to emerge from the chaos, we found that debris was strewn all over the yard, the doors and windows had been ripped off their hinges, the walls were still standing, and . . . the Germans were still there.[15]

At times, survival was nothing less than incredible. In Flers, just south of Caen, the crypt of the local church turned out to be a death trap. Janine Guérin, a seventeen-year-old bank clerk and daughter of a butcher, remembers the bombings there on the night of June 7. Her survival, she believed, was a miracle. Sadly, all her family were not so blessed.

In the morning, we heard a steady stream of loud thuds coming from the shores of the [English] Channel. We knew that the Liberation was drawing near. We had been waiting for the Allied landing for so long. At last, we would be liberated from German oppression and regain our freedom.

At 7:45 p.m. that evening, there were still quite a few people in town. It was suppertime. Out of the blue, some planes flew by and dropped bombs on rue de la Chaussée and rue de Domfront, creating a massive explosion.

We were in the delicatessen on 7 bis rue Schnetz when it happened. My mother had decided that if there was a bombing, the only dependable shelter was the crypt below Saint-Germain church. My father did not share her opinion. As it happened, rue Schnetz wasn't hit during the first bombing run. But inside the house, it was as if we were on a boat. I was on the second floor and couldn't bring myself to go downstairs. My mother had to drag me down the staircase.

When we got to the doorway, Mother said, "We really have to get to the crypt." And so we did. My father was unsure about whether to follow us. I can still picture him in his clogs and butcher coat, calmly walking up to the market square to meet us in the crypt, where we had happily taken shelter.

There were maybe several hundred of us in the crypt, with the greatest concentration of people near the entrance. Someone asked for everyone to leave the doorway clear so that people could get through. My father wanted to do something for the wounded who had begun to arrive. "We'll take a bench, put it at the back of the crypt, and we'll all sit there," he suggested. Which is what we did, except for me. I may have been more jittery than the others, I'm not sure, but I didn't want to sit down. I stood behind them.

At 8:10 p.m., three bombs hit the church. I heard a huge bang. I didn't see much—only a fiery red flash—before I was buried beneath the rubble. I heard cries and screams. There was widespread panic, but I couldn't see anything.

My father was killed instantly, and the other members of my family were seriously wounded. My brother André, who was sixteen, had a compound fracture of the thigh—with treatment, he would have survived. My mother had a bruised left arm, and her face was badly hurt. My ten-year-old brother Bernard had his head split open, his skull fractured, and his right thigh broken in two places. My fourteen-year-old sister Madeleine had a piece of shrapnel lodged in her leg and was in severe shock. Despite cracking a bone in one of her arms, the domestic took Bernard in her arms and carried him to safety. My sister pulled my mother to safety as best she could—in the crush of people, others were going over the top of them. From there, they made it to the police station on Cinqbecs square.

As for me, when everyone left I couldn't hear a thing. I knew I wasn't getting enough air and thought I'd died from asphyxiation. I didn't think they'd forgotten me, only that I was buried and they couldn't see me. At any rate, they looked back before leaving and didn't find me.

What transpired after was a miracle, I must say. Monsieur Garnier, the director of the Magasins Réunis department store in Flers, was looking for his wife. Coincidentally, she was named Alice, like my mother (not a common name). I heard him calling for Alice and thought it was my father. I couldn't breathe. Somehow, to urge him on, I summoned the inner strength to say yes. "Yes." I had the strength to say yes. Monsieur Garnier thought that it was his wife. He rushed forward and quickly unburied me from the waist up.

I was in a daze. I looked around but couldn't see anything. Then my eyes turned to Papa and my brother André, who were lying next to each other. My brother smiled heroically. He was losing blood from the wound in his thigh. He said, "Papa is dead. Save me."

My father was lying on his back. He didn't look hurt; I didn't think he was dead. I was able to free the rest of my body all on my own, although I did have trouble pulling my right leg out from the rubble. I was covered in debris. It was then that I went over to my father. My brother had told me he was dead, which was true, but for a moment I refused to believe it. My brother's plea, "Save me," will forever be in my mind. I did not save him. I was in a state of panic and did not have the wherewithal to help him.

A lot of people were going down to the crypt. From where I was on the church square, I begged everyone I saw: "Please get help!" They all promised they would, but no one ever came. Finally, stretcher bearers—I can't even remember their names—came and got my brother. It was a good thing that they did—we could have been transported elsewhere, but they took us to the police station. There I was reunited with my brother Bernard and my mother, who were both stretcher-bound. I informed my crying sister of our father's death. When Mother saw me arrive, she cried out, "Another one made it!" My father was the only one missing. Mother thought that he had been brought elsewhere. That was what we subsequently told her, that he had been wounded and that they surely had transported him to a hospital.

I also remember the joy of my brother André on his stretcher, when he recognized Raymond Burgeot. Seeing one of his classmates seemed to restore his hope. He no longer felt alone. I can still picture him after we left the Saint-Germain church crypt, looking at rue Schnetz, which hadn't been hit. I don't know exactly what was going through his mind, but my thoughts were with him.

After the police station, the doctor from Mesnil du Buisson led the wounded to Madame Décolle's home in Rainette. All the wounded were crammed into two little rooms lit by a lamp and a candle. Mother was near the window. She didn't recognize my brother André, who received several shots from the doctor. With serum, he could be saved. He was hurt a lot less badly than Bernard. We spent the night like that.

At 8:15 a.m., my brother André died. The doctor covered him up. I didn't have the strength to go see him beforehand. I remember that Mother recognized him from his breathing and moaning. "That's Dédé [André], he's here," she said. "No," we replied. We didn't have the heart to tell her.[16]

In Cherbourg some days later, Suzanne Arnault's mother placed her faith in "miraculous" medals to protect the family. The Americans had set their sights on this northern port city after establishing a successful beachhead. Between June 22 and 24, Cherbourg was also subject to fierce bombing. Like many other families, the Arnaults had built a small shelter in their backyard. It did not protect them.

The weather was very nice on Saturday, June 24. After a bit of cooking, we went back to our shelter, and the siren rang out. I climbed onto the roof of the shelter to watch the planes go by, and I saw bombs drop. "They're not very far away," I remarked. The noise was loud. Dr. Deslandes, who had gone home "to shave," was thrown all the way to the next street over; an entire block of houses was destroyed, and their street was completely blocked in by all the debris. My mother was distressed by the death of the doctor, whom she had been very fond of despite his rough exterior. She thought she was protecting herself from death by placing "miraculous" medals all over the place, both on her person and on the front door lock (which was ripped off). You could tell she was very worried.

At noon there was a short break in the mortar fire. We took the opportunity to lie down in the grass near the shelter and play a game of Dada.[17] At around 1:30 p.m., my mother told us to come back inside the shelter, because shrapnel was falling all over. She sat down with Madame Laisney in the back of the shelter. Mother knitted white cotton gloves while Madame Laisney leaned her head on Mother's shoulder and took a nap. Dimitri drew, and as for me, I read in the entrance to the shelter where there was light. A green ball appeared out of the blue. I felt a sharp pain in my eyes and couldn't hear anything around me. "Mom, I'm blind!" I screamed. But she didn't answer me. The shell had hit her head-on, and she died along with Madame Laisney. A shadow passed in front of me, and I realized that I wasn't blind. It was Dimitri, who had summoned the strength to flee despite his wounds. I later found him lying in the cellar. With the hand I still had use of (the other was slightly injured), I helped him to make a tourniquet to stanch the gushing flow of blood.

And then I went to call for help. Some people heard me, and naval firefighters arrived soon after. They realized that there was nothing they could do to save my mother and her friend, so they put Dimitri and me on stretchers (my eyes were in terrible pain), gave us a quick scrubbing at the official shelter, and then took us to the naval hospital. As I was getting down from my stretcher, a large shell hit the glass-roofed operating room. A paramedic was killed escorting other wounded. The firemen were taken by surprise and let go of my stretcher, causing me to fall onto the road. Blinded and completely overcome with fear, I began to scream. A doctor gently reasoned with me, and I quieted down.

At the time, most hospital operations were carried out underground, with a row of mattresses and small but efficient operating rooms set up in the concrete basement. . . . They washed my eyes and must have administered a sedative, because I slept for nearly twenty-four hours—up until the end of Mass celebrated right next to me without my knowing. My mattress was placed right next to a Soviet prisoner, who made some indecent proposals, one might say.[18]

Even where the Americans had triumphed, tragedy could occur. In liberated Carentan, the most unlucky of deaths happened during a ceremony honoring American heroes. Colette L'hermitte remembers the scene.

A stage was erected at place de la République in front of the war memorial to present awards to the US soldiers, who had served with valor on the battlefield. It was decorated with a blue, a white, and a red parachute. The entire civil population was invited to attend the ceremonies, which were held during the evening. I, of course, was on hand to honor our liberators, for whom we would make bouquets of flowers. This lasted until a woeful evening in late June, when a deadly shelling rained down on the square during a ceremony. Several people were wounded or killed, among them a four-year-old girl, who died instantly when a piece of shrapnel hit her directly in the heart as she handed a bouquet of flowers to an American soldier. This was the last of these ceremonies that was held; the stage was taken down the following day.[19]

A LOST SISTER

As difficult as was the fate of the Guérin and Arnault families, at least they were all together. Many other Normans were not so fortunate. A terrible anguish weighed on all those missing a loved one. Were they alive or dead? Was their house still standing? Where were they now? It was almost impossible to find out. Norman newspapers were plastered with queries about brothers, sisters, daughters, and fiancés. Radio stations featuring messages from "dispersed families" collected as many as two thousand requests a day. Desperate mothers wrote letters to mayors asking for information. Even when a Norman town had been liberated, its inhabitants were left to wonder what was going on for family elsewhere. The disappearance of his sister tormented Désiré Pottier. He felt horribly guilty that on D-Day he had not brought her back from Saint-Lô, where she worked, to the family home in Rémilly.

The aerial activity and naval artillery gradually began to die down starting at around noon. Had the landings failed? The question was running through my mind as I got on my bicycle to ride back to Saint-Lô. If the landings were over, I would have to start thinking about returning to work. When I arrived in Saint-Lô around 3:00 or 4:00 p.m., there was nary a civilian in town (perhaps fewer than twenty). There was no one in the office, either. Some policemen advised me to find somewhere to take cover; the planes had come back to bomb the train station. Where I was on rue du Neufbourg was fairly far from the station, so I didn't believe I was in danger. My earlier fear that the landings had failed now subsided—the train station and power plant were obviously bombed for a reason, which gave me hope.

Before leaving Saint-Lô, I stopped on rue Torteron to see my sister, Odette, who was sixteen at the time and working at Madame Gautier's. Odette asked me to bring her back with me, and I foolishly refused, telling her that she should continue working, because now that the train station and power plant had been taken out, there wasn't much left to bomb aside from military targets. It was a mistake that I sorely regretted that evening at around 9:00 p.m., when the first bombing of the town began. My parents and I could even hear the sound of the bombs from the courtyard of their house on rue des Vignettes, and we saw plumes of smoke billowing above Saint-Lô. It was a long night. We were very worried about my sister, even more so after I told them that she had wanted to come back, but I had told her in all honesty that she wasn't in danger. On the morning of Wednesday the seventh, we heard bad news from Saint-Lô: the city had been flattened and set ablaze. Rue Torteron was said to have been hit the hardest. So my father and I set out for Saint-Lô in search of the sister I'd left behind. It was a difficult journey—fighter planes were patrolling all the roads at low altitude, gunning down German military vehicles and anything else that moved.

For most of the way, we carried our bikes through the ditches, as the branches of the hedges afforded us cover. At last, we arrived in Agneaux. In the part of Saint-Lô below us—place des Alluvions, the neighborhood around the hospital, and rue Torteron—huge fires were raging everywhere and merging. Upon seeing the tragic sight, my father lost all hope that my sister could have somehow escaped from the hellscape. He said that he didn't want to see any more. "Go ahead if you want," he told me. "I'll wait for you, but don't do anything too risky." It wasn't possible to continue by bicycle from where we were, so I left on foot.

I made my way toward rue Torteron, but there was a point where the flames coming out of the buildings on either side of the street joined together to form an arch of fire. The heat was intense, but I had only twenty meters to go. I covered my head with my jacket and made a run for it. I dove into a hallway leading to Monsieur and Madame Gautier's house, which was near collapse. The Gautiers' home was badly damaged but still standing; the one nearest to theirs had been completely destroyed. I shouted, but no one answered. There was no way of knowing if someone was trapped under the rubble, so I decided there was no point in lingering there and returned in the opposite direction. The first time I crossed paths with someone, a member of the French Red Cross, was at the intersection in front of the hospital. He gave me some information and suggested that I go to the shelter under the boulder. The hospital management had moved most of its patients into the shelter, and many of those wounded from the bombing and other civilians had also taken refuge there. In the underground shelter, I learned that my sister had passed through earlier, but that around midnight, at the height of the bombing, all the teens sixteen and older had to leave to make room for the steady flow of wounded. So she had made it through the bombing of rue Torteron unscathed, but what had happened since? There was no one in the city—or rather what was left of it—but danger was still present in the form of time bombs that would explode here and there. . . .

We didn't find my sister or receive any information about her whereabouts. Morale was low; once again, we had no choice but to return home without her. On our way back, we met three cyclists as we rode into Montreuil. While looking for someone from Monsieur Henry's family, they had found my sister, who was with them. It was such a relief to see her—without even a scratch! She had cried nonstop since the night of the fifth–sixth out of fear and loneliness, and would cry for three more days before gradually regaining her composure after this deeply moving experience.[20]

THE FIRST GLIMPSE

At dawn on June 6, the Allies took their first steps onto beaches in the Bay of the Seine. These H-Hour invaders were infantrymen—frontline fighters—from the American, British, and Canadian armies.[1] Unlike the paratroopers, who had dropped the night before in small numbers, the infantrymen came in force. By the end of July, 1.5 million Allied soldiers would be fighting in Normandy. On beaches farther east (code-named Gold, Juno, and Sword), the British and the Canadians launched their assault. Their objective was the city of Caen, south of the beachhead. On beaches farther west (code-named Omaha and Utah), the Americans landed. Their first goal was to take the lower Cotentin and the Carentan basin.

As the day passed, Allied progress was measured in inches along some stretches of the Normandy coast. The German defenders fought doggedly from fixed positions. But by nightfall, the Americans controlled a perimeter up to a mile deep beyond Omaha Beach. This meant that French civilians in coastal towns such as Vierville and Grandcamp-les-Bains met their first American that morning.[2]

Almost everyone in Normandy remembers their first glimpse of an American. During the long years of German occupation, the Normans had imagined the moment of liberation as one of profound joy. But for civilians who found themselves in the middle of a war on June 6, that moment turned out to be quite different. First encounters happened in an atmosphere fraught with fear and danger. Language barriers fostered distrust between soldiers and civilians. Even after the Normans had been liberated, it sometimes took a while for them to realize what had happened. When the reality of their freedom began to sink in, however, they rushed to offer their liberators whatever gifts they could find.

THE PREDAWN OF LIBERATION

The predawn of liberation could be proverbially dark. As was done with the paratroopers, American infantrymen were told to use caution as they infiltrated French homes and villages. Chances of a German ambush were high, particularly in the first days of scrappy, face-to-face combat. Victorine Houyvet, a thirty-one-year-old schoolteacher in Vierville, met her first American on D-Day. Her village, steps away from Omaha Beach, was one of the first taken by the Americans that morning. Despite the virtual decimation of invaders landing on the western flank below Vierville, some men survived to reach the seawall and the town. One of them took Houyvet by surprise.

I saw my first American soldier for the first time on June 6, 1944, at about 7:00 a.m. The hallway door in the house had been blown off during the bombing, and I had had a sleepless night. I was putting on a skirt when an American showed up at the door! I didn't know that the landings were happening, because I hadn't seen any boats at sea—we couldn't see the water from the school. We had no idea. I was alone, because my colleague was upstairs. The soldier was right in front of the door but didn't enter, because he was afraid there were Germans. I was the first Frenchwoman he saw. He had just come up from the crossroads and must have taken me for a German, because he thought that all the civilians had retreated back five kilometers, and we had stayed!

He was tall—very tall—and armed like all the other soldiers. He didn't say anything; I was so bewildered that I put my hands in the air and thought to myself, *What is this beanpole doing here?* There had been plenty of talk of the landing, but we didn't think it would be at our doorstep. He took his revolver and fired, thinking I was German. Luckily, I was in front of the bedroom door and was able to get out of the way. Otherwise, he would have killed me!

The bullet flew through the window. He wouldn't cross the threshold, for fear that there were Germans inside. I can't say it was a very pleasant first encounter![3]

Many Normans emphasized the "beanpole" appearance of the Americans. Other Normans called them "giants" and "huge devils." The infantrymen could be frightening. Although their faces were not blackened like the *paras'*, they wore big helmets shadowing their foreheads and making eye contact impossible. Not being able to look her liberator in the eye panicked twenty-six-year-old farmworker Marguerite Gidon. Her first encounter with an American soldier came a few miles south of Vierville, in Bernesq, on June 10. Like many other Normans, she was liberated while caught in a cross fire.

I saw my first American on Saturday, June 10. It was about 6:30 in the morning, and twenty-two of us were in a trench. We had a little three-month-old baby with us, who was crying because he was hungry and his mother was so terrified that she didn't have any more milk. So we fed the little kid sugar water, but he still cried quite often, so I took him into my arms. I was on the edge of the trench when, much to my surprise, an American arrived. His face was hidden by his helmet and netting. He had a gun and was dressed in green—what an awful green! I was so scared that I dropped the little baby! He fell onto the straw in the trench.

The soldier waved us over and explained that others were on

their way. When we got out of the trench, we saw about fifteen soldiers, and we understood why. At that very moment, we had been liberated: we wanted to laugh, we wanted to cry—we felt relieved. But we were in the bend, caught in the cross fire: the Germans (or the Boches, as we called them at the time) were running away, and the Americans were landing. They were shooting at each other, so we stayed hidden in the trenches.

We offered him something to drink, but he didn't want to straightaway. We had to drink first for him to accept! He was afraid that we were trying to poison him! He ended up taking a drink, then gave the packs of cigarettes he had in his pockets to the men in the trench.[4]

The GIs feared that those civilians left in coastal towns, largely evacuated by the Germans, were collaborators protected by the enemy. Afraid of being poisoned by Nazi sympathizers, they made civilians drink anything offered them.

The same day, June 10, nineteen-year-old Jacques Bailleul also had a frightening first encounter with an American. His GI was operating a tank, and aimed its gun turret directly at him.

It was the morning of June 10, at the far end of town near the road to Saint-Martin de Blagny. First I saw an American vehicle, a sort of armored vehicle, a little tank, if you will. It struck me as odd, surely because the previous evening, the Germans were still here! They had taken up a position in town, before heading up to the woods behind the chateau; we heard them in the embankments and the hollows. Late at night, we heard a rally cry, and the German horse-drawn carriages left—as did the men, who retreated posthaste!

And that morning, that tank was there, waiting on the road at the outskirts of the woods! I thought it was alone. I hesitated, unsure of what was happening . . . was there a cross on it, where is the German cross? The tank was intriguing, especially the strange packs on it.

I didn't really have a clue what was going on—it all went so fast! When I arrived, it turned its gun turret!

But at the time, I still hadn't seen anyone. I went back to my house and told the others what was going on; then several of us went back to see. I was with my brothers and people from town who had been forced to leave because of the bombings, as well as a young mining engineer; there were no fewer than fifteen of us in all.

Then the tank did it again—it pointed its gun at us—and we still couldn't see anyone; there was only the sound of the radio. So we quietly went on our way toward the field, because, well, we were afraid and didn't know what was happening.

We continued down in that direction, and upon arrival discovered that we were surrounded by Americans. They were so quiet, dressed in camouflage and wearing rubber boots (unlike the Germans, who made a lot of noise at night). They were as silent as could be, but there were hundreds of them, and they were pointing their weapons at us. The column readied itself and deployed, keeping an eye on us all the while (we were at the outskirts of the woods). Each time a soldier advanced, a sergeant would stop and cover him, and the men would run forward.

The soldiers were covered with black smears, and their helmets and clothes were camouflaged with foliage. They looked a little strange—stressed and wary, very wary—but more than anything they looked scary, with their knives and packs of clips, not to mention the huge magazines on their rifles. Some even had bloodstains on their uniforms, and others were soaked to the waist!

At first we didn't really communicate much, but we did a few hours later, when the first group had already left. That's when it sank in and we said, "This is it! We've been liberated!" We finally really believed it. It was the real thing.[5]

American combat boots were a thing of wonder to the Normans. In contrast to the German boots, which made loud clickety-clack sounds on the cobblestone, the American variety was rubber-soled and quiet as a cat.

Once the Americans had gained a foothold around the beaches, all attention was focused on Cherbourg, at the tip of the Cotentin Peninsula. A natural harbor, the city could provide the Allies with a major port from which to unload men and materiel. As the V and VII Corps moved west and then north toward Cherbourg, the fearful predawn of liberation kept happening.

Jean Roy of Vauville, west of Cherbourg, had another reason to be frightened when he saw his first American soldier: he mistook him for a German. Roy had refused to do compulsory labor for the Nazis. Toward the end of the war, the occupiers seized able-bodied men on the street and sent them to factories in Germany. Roy had somehow escaped that fate and was officially in hiding.

The two Germans who were guarding the munitions shed would cross the courtyard every morning to fetch milk. At eight o'clock in the morning on June 19 or 20, one of them came into the house, panicked, and said, "Big trouble . . . Tommies[6] in Briquebec." An hour later, Rémy Sanson, who must have been around ten years old, arrived at the house and told us, "The Americans are in Haut de Biville. There were only two jeeps. They were asking where the Boches were. One climbed to the top of a telephone pole and cut the wires." Uncle Michel took Rémy on his cart to go back to see "The Americans." But he didn't see anything, because the Americans had fallen back.

A little before noon, when Uncle had returned, I set out to find my grandmother, Marie Sanson, in Vinebus. I had only just left when I saw the first American soldier. I was scared and considered turning back. I didn't recognize the uniform straightaway and thought he might be a German soldier searching for young people (I had refused to do Compulsory Work Service!). But I was too close to him, so I continued on my way. That was when I noticed there really were Americans, a group about thirty meters in front of the first one, marching in two columns on either side of the road. We crossed paths; I was walking in the middle of the road, and we studied each other without exchanging a word or gesture.[7]

After the Germans surrendered Cherbourg on June 26, the Americans turned their sights southward. But their progress in the first half of July was frustratingly slow. The Norman landscape, with its fields divided by tall, impenetrable hedgerows, favored the defenders and made forward movement nearly impossible for heavy artillery and tanks. German snipers were also a huge problem. They would remain behind after the German soldiers retreated, hiding in the hedgerows and picking off American soldiers one by one. When they were at last out of ammunition and food, they would emerge to surrender. Even if the Germans had left a town, sniper fire could come from anywhere anytime. In Jean-Jacques Vautier's first glimpse of the Americans, we can see the GIs remaining always on alert for snipers.

Around 11:30 a.m., a shout rang out: "They're here!" Sure enough, we could hear a steady rumble coming from the road. We stood on the roadside, our hearts thumping, and a helmet appeared at the top of the hill, followed by more helmets, and a car. The convoy made its way down slowly. When the first vehicle—a scout car or something of the sort—rolled past us, we all burst out in cheers. A lady threw a bouquet. The leader of the group stood stern and alert, making the V sign with his hands. Seated beside him on the tracked truck, the soldiers kept their guns trained on the side of the road, their finger on the trigger, ready to fire. They made the

V with their right hand, without letting go of their rifle. Their ash- and dust-covered faces showed signs of fatigue; their eyes shone brightly. Their silence kept us quiet; we understood them.[8]

By mid-July, the Norman terrain had created a war hell for the Allies. In twelve days of battle that summer, VIII Corps suffered ten thousand casualties to take seven miles of territory.[9] Hedgerow fighting was also hard on the soul: that month, one of every four infantry casualties in the 21st Army Group was for combat exhaustion or shell shock.[10] In response to this near stalemate, General Omar Bradley devised Operation Cobra, a breakthrough plan that combined massive air bombardment and concentrated attack. Launched on July 24 west of Saint-Lô, the campaign was a success, and allowed the penetration of US forces south and west toward Rennes and Brittany.

But the transition from war to peace remained dangerous. In the town of Fleury, southwest of Saint-Lô, Christiane Denis experienced his liberation, once again, as a moment of terror. The turning point for him was seeing a yellow banner flying above a plane nearby. American infantrymen used yellow panels in order to identify their positions to Air Force personnel and to prevent friendly fire.

I had learned from experience that the little paths weren't safe, for a sentry could mistake me for an enemy. It was seven o'clock in the morning (local sun time). Through the gate, I caught a glimpse of a soldier with an odd look about him: small, stocky, and sharp-eyed, he had a five o'clock shadow and dirty clothes. He didn't at all look like a Boche, but not for one second did I think he could be American. Two others appeared at the gate. I didn't know whether to keep walking forward or to turn around. He gestured for me to come over, and as I approached he said, "American." I must confess that I was crying tears of joy as I wrapped my arms around him.

Using a small book of phrases, he was able to ask me if there were any Boches in the region. I told him I hadn't a clue, but that if he wished, I could find out and pass on the information to him. He accepted, and it was decided that I'd come back to meet him half an hour later.

I first went over to Gastebled's place—if there were any left in the area, they were bound to be there. Two had eaten there but had since moved on.[11] To appear to be going about my business, I headed toward the bakery. But before I could get there, I crossed paths with Marcel René, who confirmed that there weren't any more Germans in town. So I turned back and talked to a few more people along the way. It was clear that the Boches were gone. There was no one at the meeting point when I arrived; I was afraid that I'd gotten there late. I let out a little shout, and one of them appeared. After I explained the situation, he frowned at me and cast a leery glare. I made a gesture to reassure him I was telling the truth. Then he slung his weapon over his shoulder, took me by the arm, and signaled for me to follow him. My blood ran cold; I had the very distinct impression of having fallen into a trap. *These so-called Americans are nothing but Germans*, I thought to myself. I was a dead man. I gathered my senses and walked beside him. He tried to give me some chocolate, but I scornfully refused. We walked 130 meters together, him upright like a Boche and me with a single thought on my mind: end this as quickly as possible. At a bend in the path, I caught sight of a yellow banner flying above an airplane on the road at Chênaie junction. I had a new lease on life. My friend—for I could call him that now—had me explain all that I knew to an interpreter, who then transmitted the information to an officer. . . . I couldn't wait to share the good news, so I went back to Poulain Street. All those brave souls were still in the stable, silent. As I opened the door I told them, "Stand up! We're American!" It is difficult to express how much those four words can change the life of a community after such trying times. Everyone wanted to go have a look, but I assured them that we were almost certainly saved. We weren't completely in the clear—it would have been crazy to ruin the happy moment out of carelessness. I got permission to bring a few treats to our liberators. I took them a bottle of Calvados and some other things.[12]

The range of emotions felt by Denis in this incident captures the mood of these first encounters. Bernard Gourbin beautifully describes the transition from terror to euphoria that could occur, sometimes in a matter of minutes.

The first American soldier slowly approached our dining room window. Beads of sweat were running down his grim face. He took aim at us, and once he was sure there were only civilians, he continued on his way, still on his guard. The second gave us a stone-faced look. The third winked at us. The following ones said "Hello" or "Good morning," hugged us, and said, "Merci!" For the tenth, we took out a bottle of cider. A few dozen later, and we had moved on to the Calvados!

This impromptu welcome was a joyful, exuberant experience that lasted quite a long time: at least one hour, but in truth probably closer to two—you don't notice the passage of time during these sorts of moments. It's hard to describe the immense joy we felt. After all this time, I still get chills thinking about it. At first we were in disbelief: we were liberated, do you realize that? Lib-er-at-ed! Words of warmth and kindness poured out of our mouths in praise of our liberators. It's difficult to express in words, even today.[13]

LANGUAGE BARRIERS

The first frightful moments of liberation eventually gave way to unmitigated joy. Nevertheless, communication remained a problem. If Christiane Denis got a "leery glare" from an American soldier when he offered information, most likely it resulted from miscomprehension. More than any other factor, the language barrier between soldier and civilian fostered mutual doubt. Very few GIs spoke French. And even those Normans with years of schooling in English could not really understand their liberators. Marcel Leveel's first encounter with an American in Lison, just south of Omaha Beach, demonstrates how that inability to communicate kindled distrust. The American *yeah* sounded very much like the German *ja*, which led some civilians to confuse Germans and Americans.

It was 8:00 a.m. when a figure appeared at the top of the hill, near the house in ruins that belongs to Leboidre. The man, who was alone, bent over and paused for a moment, then continued toward us. Bottle of cider in hand, Albert and I went to meet him. In my head, I went over the sentence I was planning to say to him. However, my English was very poor, and I didn't have my dictionary. We crossed paths one hundred meters from the house, in front of Monot's place. He stopped and, using pliers,[14] appeared to cut the wire running along the side of the road. He was holding a telephone and had a big leather bag slung over his shoulder. He wasn't very tall, and his face was hidden by his enormous helmet. He had a dark complexion. He barely turned his head when we arrived.

"We are Frenchmen, and we are your friends."

But he ignored us completely and continued working.

"I have studied English at school. I speak some words only. Do you understand me?"

"Yeah, yeah."

Hey, he speaks German to say yes! I showed him the bottle of cider and asked, "Drink?"

He shook his head no. We were a bit disconcerted. I pointed to the wire and asked, "No good?"

He replied something that I didn't understand and then left, continuing downhill. Part of the family was waiting for us at our gate. He had a gun that looked like a rifle. I didn't know what more to say. I tried to find his rank or a badge, but there was nothing!

"You are not sirty?"

We walked close to him. I gestured with my thumb for him to take a drink. Sign language is a good language!

"Ah, thirsty! No."

Communication was difficult, just like with his telephone.

Everyone was waiting for him at the gate of the house.

"He's no fun at all. He's like the ones that passed through last night: testy."

We had barely stepped in the door when, late in the afternoon, a patrol of seven or eight men headed up the hill.

"Bring a bottle . . . no, two, there are a lot of them."

"Hello!"

We had learned by that time that they said hello.

"Alors, comment ça va?" one of them asked. Surprisingly, he spoke French, with a strange accent.

"Are there any Boches around here?"

His use of the term *Boche* surprised us. Another mentioned cognac. We gave them some cider, which was not to their liking. We were, of course, required to take a drink first. My mother suggested opening a bottle of wine, which they enjoyed. One of them gave me some cigarettes, and left the pack. The tobacco tasted wonderful. The case was red and made of cardboard. According to what was written, the flavor was Egyptian![15] . . . And for the first time, I heard the famous "OK" that I knew to be typically American.[16]

The young daughter of Norman farmers, Yvette Travert also recalled trouble communicating on D-Day, but in this case it did not seem to matter.

"Look who's coming, smoking cigarettes. Why, we know those two brothers. Have you seen the Americans?"

"Why, yes, they are 150 meters from you," they replied.

There were eighteen of us, and not a single one stayed put. Everyone started running, racing to see who would get there first. The tanks turned in our direction and aimed their turrets at us. Beside them were a couple of jeeps and about thirty soldiers on the alert.

"We're only the front line," explained one of the soldiers, who spoke a bit of French. Locals, out-of-towners, and refugees—everyone surrounded them, embraced them, and showered them with flowers. A few people broke down in front of these big, stoic guys with tanned faces and shaved heads, who were visibly tired. The soldiers didn't speak our language and remained silent. Even the well-known collaborators gathered with the crowd—it was abhorrent.

Two regiments passed by us in single file. The scout returned to his duties as well, after saying goodbye. A little jeep stopped in front of the house to ask for directions. There was the driver, a colonel, and a general. They had very few decorations; the general was as simply dressed as the driver. We talked a bit, and my sisters, who had just milked the cows, offered the men some milk, which they gratefully accepted.

Some of the chattier folks asked them a bunch of questions in French and *patois* that they were not able to answer. One brave man tried a few words of German from his repertoire. They didn't understand that, either.

There was a tremendous feeling of joy, of unbridled elation. It didn't matter that we didn't understand exactly why: we were friends, allies . . . we were buddies![17]

Note how Travert refers to the collaborators. Welcoming the Americans became a way for those who had done business with the Germans to cloak their sympathies. But in small villages, everyone knew *who* had done *what*. Travert also points out something about the US Army that puzzled Normans. The lack of insignia on the

American uniform made it difficult for them to figure out who were the officers and who were the enlisted men.

A young Jacques Petit, refugee from Saint-Lô, was another who found that his school English did not help him much when he was liberated on August 2.

Near the farm, Sherman tanks were lined up along the hedges. I attempted to strike up a conversation with their occupants. So what exactly was the language the men in khaki spoke? I was proficient in Shakespeare and had been collecting first prizes in English for the past six years. That evening, I was able to string together a few intelligible sentences once I had gathered some momentum, but I didn't understand a single word of their rapid-fire answers![18]

How grateful the Normans were when a GI could speak French! The Ferrarys from Grandchamp-les-Bains remember being thankful to a New Yorker whose father was French.

We had quickly taken shelter behind a section of wall in a half-demolished house when we saw a group of American soldiers advancing silently in their rubber-soled boots. They were dressed in khaki jackets, pants, and gaiters, knives at their waist and light rifle or submachine gun in hand. They moved with the phenomenal litheness of big cats in the jungle or Indians on the warpath.

The soldiers were covered in dust and mud. They had the weathered faces of men who had been fighting since the landing—on the edge of minefields and roads blown away by German fire—and who were no strangers to fierce hand-to-hand combat. They moved forward step by step, in short bursts from one roadside ditch to another, under the protection of their fearsome artillery and vast air support. . . .

There was a chill as night fell. My companions shivered in the biting north wind, and the wait became protracted.

We again signaled our presence. A soldier gestured to us, and we formed a group. He led us to a house near the new church, where a few people from Grandcamp had gathered before the battle because of its particularly secure cellar under the cubic construction of its pristine white walls.

The American guard in front of the door was an exceedingly handsome man. He was of average height, with a very dark complexion and fine features. His father was French, but he was born in New York. Morel was his name. He showed us the Cross of Lorraine[19] pinned to the inside of his jacket.

"I wanted to fight in France," he explained, "and joined the commandos so that I could be in one of the companies that stormed the beaches."

"Your wish must have been granted, because you're here now!"

He smiled. Overcome with emotion, we took his hands and expressed our gratitude that he and the others had traveled so far to free us from our bonds.[20]

"WE WERE ALL AMERICANS!"

Particularly after the Americans broke out of the hedgerows south and west of Saint-Lô in late July, the fate of the battle was less held in the balance. A ritual was soon established in French villages: the GIs were welcomed with flowers, cheers, and warm smiles. Here is how René Doucloue, a refugee from Saint-Lô, remembers the joyful moment on July 28, 1944:

Suddenly and without fanfare, the Germans left. They turned their backs to the sea. We were certain that others would come to relieve them, but much to our surprise, none did. Were they really gone? When we ventured out to their positions in the early afternoon, we saw that they had been abandoned. There was not a German in sight. We wanted to shout, "It's true, they're really gone!" But the same thing had happened in Sainteny: they left, and the town was bombed all the same.

Then around 5:00 p.m. we heard the sound of engines, of tracked vehicles, coming from the town. This was followed by cries of joy and men, women, and children descending on the town. So we decided to join them in seeing what was going on.

What was going on was that the Americans had arrived. They were on the road, right before our eyes. They paraded past us in their beige vehicles with a big white star on the side: tankettes, half-tracks, trucks, jeeps, and tanks. The entire town was there; I'd say over a thousand people lined up to watch the convoy roll by. The convoy stopped, and the Americans shook hands with people and handed out cigarettes (my brother got one) and even packs of cigarettes (my father was lucky enough to catch one). The soldiers were showered with flowers and hastily prepared bouquets of flowers. They were given bottles of wine that had been successfully hidden from the Germans. French flags appeared in windows, and church bells pealed out. Joy, celebration, and jubilation filled the air: we had regained our freedom! Yes, we had been liberated! . . . That night we were all Americans![21]

The Americans were big, smart, good-looking, and rich. That's what Abbé Dufour thought when he saw his first GI in Lorey, southwest of Saint-Lô, on the twenty-eighth of July.

Right on schedule, at 8:00 a.m., we began to hear an increasingly loud noise from the direction of Étretat. It could only be one thing: our liberators, speeding down in an armored column. I had been waiting a few minutes near the north end of the cemetery, when a jeep appeared at the lower end of town and drove up the hill toward me. It stopped in front of me, and an officer got out and put out his hand. Flustered, I could only manage, "Welcome, you are welcome." He answered in halting but cordial French, "Very well, you, Monsieur le

Pasteur, are the first in the village to welcome the Americans." I was moved by this small compliment, which I think was well deserved! The officer then asked me various questions and had me walk with him to the wayside shrine. The armored detachment congregated there, about twenty vehicles in all: jeeps, trucks, armored cars, and light tanks. The soldiers aboard were strapping fellows, let me tell you. I had never seen any others like them, even among the occupiers. They were camouflaged, as were their vehicles, with netting and branches. From first sight, they exuded power . . . and confidence.[22]

Even the presence of looters at his house the next day did not sour Dufour's opinion of the Americans.

The night was calm and relaxing—peace at last after all that commotion! I'm sad to say that my day was more than infuriating. Last Thursday, the Germans looted me "neatly," in a manner of speaking, and without breaking anything inside my house. The same cannot be said for what happened today. After leaving the rectory one last time for luncheon, I came back at 4:00 p.m. to find my room in a pitiful state. From my window, I caught a glimpse of two Americans "visiting" Arthémise Vigot and Marcel Marion's house, while a third waited outside in the road. I went up to the third soldier and reprimanded him harshly, making him summon the two others. But it was no use: they swore they weren't the "gangsters" I was looking for. And after all, this was nothing compared with all the ruin and misery of the war: my house was still standing! All the same, that wasn't a reason to clear the guilty of wrongdoing, and I know that during that time, in Lorey, there were other looters than the Germans and the Americans. Out of kindness, I won't elaborate!

We ended the evening in my house and garden with a charming group of American soldiers with whom I had a long and enjoyable conversation. They promised me chocolate, candy, etc. Two days later, they kept their word, and in return I gave them some "cogna" [cognac]—they are fond of that—and there are no hard feelings on my part![23]

Young boys and girls particularly admired the Americans. Claude Bourdon, fourteen at the time of the Liberation, remembers the exciting day the Americans finally arrived in his town southeast of Saint-Lô. He wrote to his diary on August 7:

They're here at last! Praised be God! After four long years of waiting, our liberators were on their way. . . . In the blink of an eye, everyone with bicycles rushed to them, while others raced to the road on foot. Papa took my bike, so I got on the luggage rack. After a little ways, I saw clouds of smoke. I kept kicking my poor father to make him go faster. Then a strange sensation came over me, and my heart started pounding. I was at the point of breaking into sobs of joy. The "Yankees" were in sight. I walked up to a car with three of them inside, one of whom had such a pretty face and beautiful eyes that I couldn't help but stare. The driver looked like a nice fellow. I saw that he had taken an interest in me, with my "American look." I didn't waste any time striking up a "conversation" of gestures.

Charmed by my company, at the end of our conversation he gave me some "swing-gamme" [chewing gum], and I gave him a rose. He put it to his nose and then fastened it to his buttonhole. After a few more chats, it was time for them to leave. Goodbyes and farewells were exchanged pell-mell, along with the two-fingered V sign for "victory." I gave a firm "sake-hand" [handshake] to the two men in the jeep, sad to see them go. Oh well, there will be others! As they started on their way, the thirty-strong convoy was showered with flowers, goodbyes, and cries of "Well good!" We headed back home, our hearts filled with immense joy. I chewed "his" gum. . . . When we arrived, the mayor's son announced that he was giving an all-night dance to celebrate their arrival. I danced with Monsieur

Lesage and his brother-in-law, but I would have preferred to dance with the Americans. Oh well, I'll get my chance. Papa delivered a baby that very night![24]

American technology completely wowed the Normans. The jeeps, the tanks, the telephones! Yvette Travert remembered how "with the help of a French-English phrasebook, one of them explained the purpose of all the weapons that stood before me. They had machine guns, submachine guns, knives—you name it—they even had mine detectors and radio transmitters. It really was a modern war."[25] Albert Desile was particularly puzzled by the telephones. In his diary of August 3, he wrote:

As we were leaving the café on the square, a strange automobile drove up in a hurry and pulled over under the trees. Inside were four soldiers dressed in khaki, wearing helmets covered in green netting. It was the Americans! One of the men, a short, brown-haired man with a thin black mustache, stood up, picked up a telephone handset, and began to speak as he studied a map. The scene struck me as odd: an almost square car with a built-in telephone—without a wire! A crowd of curious onlookers quickly gathered. We remained silent for a moment, almost dumbfounded, then all of a sudden it dawned on us what the presence of American soldiers actually meant. It was pandemonium! A chorus of cries broke out: "Vive l'Amérique!" "Vive la France!" "Vive de Gaulle!"[26]

LETTUCE AND CALVA

Grateful for their liberation, the Normans emerged bearing gifts. Because they were not rich folk, these offerings were humble and improvised. Jean Roy's present to the GIs turned out to be the lettuce his grandmother had given him from her garden.

When I came back to Le Fief, I found the Americans there waiting. They were strong in numbers and armed with guns and grenades. Some of them sat smoking near the wall. When they saw me arrive with my basket, some of them started talking to me. But I didn't understand what they were saying. Then one of them pointed to the basket with the lettuce. I understood and gave it to them, which made them happy. And it made me happy to please them. They pulled off the outside leaves and eagerly ate the heart. And that was how my grandmother's lettuce was eaten. They may not have had any fresh food for a long time. Afterward, an American who spoke a little French asked me, "How many kilometers to Cherbourg?" They left that afternoon. They looked exhausted.[27]

Janine Chambrin was eleven years old at the time. She remembers the presents she gave—and refused to give—to her first American soldiers in Vierville, near the landing beaches.

I first saw and met American soldiers on June 6, 1944, but I'm not sure what time it was. I didn't really think about the time of day; it was surely in the afternoon, I was in the yard with my parents. There had been some heavy bombing, after which we went to stay in the covered shelter, with the horses and the Germans who were guarding them. . . . My father, who had left in search of news, caught sight of soldiers on the road that he mistook for Germans. One of the soldiers who was staying at the house—the Germans had commandeered several rooms—went into the courtyard, and the soldiers in the street shot at him. My father realized they were American and went over to them and said, "My entire family is in the shelter."

They came to get us in the shelter; unfortunately, I don't have a very good recollection of the Americans or our conversation, because I was so young. But I do remember that a little while later, my mother picked a rose for me and sent me to give it to one of the soldiers as a welcome gift, a way to greet them and give thanks.

I remember that a few days later, a soldier wanted me to give him the little rosary that I had on a tiny doll that was meant to be a girl taking Communion. The Communion had been held in Vierville on Sunday, as it happened, and the landing took place the following Tuesday. I had taken my first Communion that Sunday and was given the doll and the rosary, and I just couldn't give it away! I was too young to understand. Later, I would come to very much regret it.

The night of the landing, the first thing the Americans gave us was a bar that looked like a chocolate bar, which they urged us to eat, saying, "Nervous! Nervous! Nervous!" My mother didn't want me to have any, because she thought it was a sort of drug used to give soldiers a boost during the war and make them fearless and brave.[28]

A little while later we went into the American sector, where we were showered with all sorts of gifts: canned pineapple and other fruit, cartons of cigarettes, chocolates, etc. A real cornucopia of goodies! . . . We offered them Calvados, which they as Americans weren't familiar with, and they downed their glass like it was wine—they nearly choked![29]

Many an American soldier choked when he took his first slug of Calvados, a strong brandy made of local apples. *Calva*, as it was called, became a popular form of money in the first weeks of the invasion. Farmers traded this regional specialty for soap, rations, and gasoline. But in the first days, it was offered as a gift. Much laughter resulted when the GIs attempted to drink it down like any other drink. Abbé Georges Cadel tells the story of another American taking his first swig of *calva*.

On Friday morning, on a farm a few kilometers west of Coutances, we saw the Germans hurriedly leave the area where they had been stationed for a few weeks, taking all their gear with them. At around eleven o'clock at night, the dogs started barking ferociously. We caught sight of some shadows on the porch.

A woman went to see who was there. She pointed her electric lamp at the group. They were soldiers. They quickly seized her hand to put out the light.

"Your friends, gone this morning," she said to them. "No one here. If you want to sleep, there is a stable with straw."

We were surprised by the fact that the soldiers didn't respond at all, not even in monosyllabic words or broken French, as they often would.

So she continued, asking, "You Georgian Russians?" No response. "You Germans?" Still nothing. She ventured a last guess, "You Americans?"

"A-mer-i-cans, yes!" a tall soldier finally replied, his hand on his heart.

The news soon spread throughout the house: "The Americans are here!" The farmer got up and ran out wearing only pants. Sparkling cider and Calvados were quickly brought out to celebrate their arrival, much to everyone's delight. One of them wasn't very accustomed to our brandy and swallowed it down like milk. He burned his throat and stuck his tongue out in a comical fashion, drawing laughter from everyone there, himself included. We wanted to prepare a place for them to stay, but after the drinks the soldiers decided to dig little trenches in the neighboring fields and sleep there. . . .

The next day, in another village, an old man had his first meal with the Americans. What a difference there was between their snow-white bread and the black bread mixed with chopped straw available to the civilian population! An NCO [noncommissioned officer] noticed the man's astonishment, and gave him a big hunk. Tears filled his eyes and he hugged the American, who exclaimed, "Ah, Papa!" Then the old man ran back to his house to hand out this wonderful gift of "sacred bread" to everyone in the house and his neighbors.[30]

Normans usually ate brown rather than white bread. White flour was relatively unknown in the region and considered a delicacy. During the war, all flour was very scarce, so bakers put in "fillers" such as hay. Besides *calva*, the Normans could offer a home-cooked meal. Chicken was a lip-smacking favorite, as well as bread, eggs, cheese, or any fresh food unavailable at the local PX. The boys became experts at "dropping by" houses during mealtimes. The Normans were willing and often eager to share. Madame Marie Jeanne Leneveu, eighteen years old in 1944, remembers how much the GIs loved her mother's cooking.

I can't remember exactly when I saw an American soldier for the first time. It was right after the landing, but the memory is vague; I can't remember what day it was. But I know it was in the afternoon, in La Folie, with my parents and brothers. I had just finished class, and the Americans were making their way down through the pasture. They didn't have the same helmets as the Germans; theirs were khaki, and they had white tunics with a colorful leaf pattern so that they would go unnoticed by passing airplanes. We were happy to see them, to be liberated. They gave us coffee and hot chocolate mix and things like that. All that we had to offer was cider and Calvados.

I can remember certain names: there was one who was called "Jostapisky" and another named "Roswesfid" who was killed in Saint-Lô. One evening, Mother made him chicken. He told us, "I've got to go kill some Germans with my knife in Saint-Lô!" and he never came back.

There was one who was in the First Army, the "shock troops" (they were the first to pass through town). He had been moved there for having punched his superior; his punishment was a transfer to the "shock troops."[31] He was killed in Saint-Lô.

It lasted pretty much all summer, us having the Americans. They were bursting with energy and in good spirits, especially "Roswesfid." I remember that he would often say, "*Maman*, good cook," to compliment Mother's cooking. What they really liked was the Calvados. In the beginning, they didn't know what *calva* was—it was really strong, and they would down a little glass in one go! They discovered Calvados and brought a little bit back with them.[32]

Normans like Madame Leneveu knew that the GI she was feeding that night might in fact be eating his last good meal. Her first glimpse of an American would often be her last. To Madame Mahier, a gift of farmhouse bread was all the more meaningful for this reason.

Some soldiers, shock troops I think, were lying down on the sidewalk, using their helmets as pillows. From what we could understand, not speaking their language, they hadn't slept for eight days after leaving Barneville. I was very happy to be able to offer them a big slice of farmhouse bread with a dab of butter. I knew they enjoyed it, because we were lucky enough to at least have bread, brought to us in the shelter by the baker, Madame Groult, despite the air raid warnings. Sometimes I think about this small group of soldiers stretched out on the sidewalk, how many lived to see their country again, and how many fell in the abundant fields of wild daisies that covered our countryside in the summer of 1944.[33]

CHAPTER FIVE

SHARING A BATTLEFIELD

In the summer of 1944, Normans watched their backyards turn into a theater of war. The Overlord plan was to liberate Normandy in three weeks. Instead, it took three months. For those twelve weeks, Normans lived between the two most powerful armies ever assembled. It was a huge transition for them. Before the landings, Normandy had been a pastoral land of fields, cows, and farmhouses. Dairy products—milk, butter, Camembert cheese—were the local pride. In a matter of hours, that landscape changed dramatically. Picturesque church steeples became sniper posts. Barns hid stockpiles of ammunition. Hedgerows sheltered artillery. As their fields became battlefields, tens of thousands of Normans took to the road, migrating all over France. Departure was rushed and chaotic. But despite their haste, Normans could not elude the fighting. Nor did they escape the corpses or the sight of GIs suffering wounds, exhaustion, or hysteria. Death was everywhere that summer. Even children were witness to its sights and smells. Sharing a battlefield meant sharing sorrow as well as danger. Normans tried to help in whatever way they could.

IN THE CROSS FIRE

Families living south of the beaches suddenly found themselves in a cross fire. Such was the case of the Darondels, whose farm was located in Formigny, steps away from Omaha Beach. Because of the Darondels' proximity to the shore, their farm suffered bombardment from both airplanes and naval artillery. The farm also lay in the footpath of the American advance during the invasion's first hours. As a result, on the Wednesday and Thursday after D-Day, Monsieur Darondel had a stream of guests in his farmhouse: first German soldiers, then American soldiers, then the Germans once again.

On Tuesday, the sixth of June, at 3:30 in the morning, I heard the distant sound of airplanes. At this very moment, I saw the first American plane in flames and falling to the ground toward Surrain. I went to see it, but I was not able to get close due to the explosions. On the road home, I saw two of my horses in a pasture, one mortally wounded and the other resting on its side and copiously bleeding. It was time for me to go home, because naval artillery was shooting from all directions. The planes cut across the sky, and German anti-aircraft artillery furiously retaliated.

At this moment, dawn broke. I led four horses back into the stable. Then my family and I took refuge in a makeshift shelter to await events. From this point onward, we were aware of the danger at hand; we understood that finally, the Allies had landed.

On Wednesday morning, the seventh of June, we were able to do the farm chores and milk the cows, at least until 9:00 a.m. After that hour, we heard the naval cannons booming without stop. From a window in the attic, we could see the bombs falling on Trevières, whose houses were in flames. All around us crackled gunfire and the firing of machine guns.

In a moment of calm, around one o'clock in the afternoon, I looked out the door and saw soldiers coming down along the hedges of the large pastures, which are to the right of my driveway and lead up from the sea. After observing them for a few seconds, I realized that these soldiers were not Germans but Americans.

When I signaled them, they made a sign for me to go inside, then fell back, their reconnaissance evidently finished.

After a brief meal, I decided to do my own reconnaissance. Following the direction of the American soldiers, taking care, and crawling with a white handkerchief in my hand, I headed toward the place where I thought I might find them in the field I named "Le Plant." There, in fact, I found about fifteen large tanks and fifty men. Some of them put up their guns, signaling me to advance toward them while aiming at me. The guard took me to his captain, who spoke French. Out of prudence, he made me lie down, and I noticed that all the soldiers who were not on guard were also lying down, very calmly eating or smoking. Then the captain asked me: "Who are you?" I told him I was the owner of the neighboring farm, which he could see himself from where he was standing. He followed this answer with a set of questions: What did I know of the Germans? Where were they? What were their numbers and their armament? I told him all this information. When I had told him what I knew, I asked him to spare my farm, since there were neither soldiers nor armament present there. He promised me this, and he kept his word. I drank with him an excellent cup of coffee, something which I had not had for several years. Then I found myself stuffing my pockets with cigarettes. Finally, the captain said to me: "To my great regret I am obliged to keep you here, because I don't know you. I suppose you are a good Frenchman, but if it was otherwise, you would be able to tell the Germans our location." He had me evacuated toward Surrain with a large number of the inhabitants of this hamlet. The American advance continued, as did the battle. We remained at Surrain until the next day at noon.

Meanwhile, my wife stayed at the farm with our two children and the servants. During this time she was visited by an American patrol, whose chief entered the house. He asked her where the Germans were. She responded that they surrounded the farm and were clearly visible, as they were only about one hundred meters away. The American declared he wanted to kill them "in order to avenge his buddies now dead on the sand." Before leaving, he left a packet of cigarettes and some candy on the table. He advised my wife to stay in the house, insisting that he would return in the evening.

About a half hour later, armed German soldiers took their turn coming to the farm in order to ask for provisions. To get rid of them, my wife gave them milk and cider. Such comings and goings continued all afternoon, provoking my wife's fear that a meeting between German and American soldiers would occur and lead to a battle on the farm. All while the Germans came for provisions, walking or crawling on all fours, the tanks located on "Plant" did not stop firing. Around 9:00 p.m., the firing did stop. The chief of the American patrol came back and asked my wife if she had seen the Germans again, and what their location was. She responded affirmatively, and indicated the place where they were sheltered. The chief left in the direction of the tanks, and the firing started again full blast until one o'clock in the morning. At this moment, the battle came closer, and face-to-face combat began. The next morning, a German soldier, carrying a machine gun, came again for provisions. He declared that out of forty, thirty-seven of his comrades had been killed. "C'est la guerre," my wife responded. He then said to her: "Madame, a big battle will take place here soon, and the Tommies go to the sea." Then he left the Costils. It was at this time that I came back, happy to find everyone in good health and the farm undamaged.

One more time we were forced to receive a visiting German soldier. It was Thursday evening, around five o'clock. I asked him the news of the battle. He was distraught, like a tracked animal. He begged us to tell him where he could go to save himself without meeting the Tommies, who were arriving everywhere. I advised him to surrender, but he and his two comrades fell back toward

Trévières. Without a doubt they were throwing themselves into the mouth of a wolf, as Trévières was completely surrounded.[1]

Young Christine Fenand also lived just south of the landing beaches, near Mandeville-en-Bessin. On June 8, she, too, found herself between American and German lines. As she told her diary that day:

There were about twenty-five of us lying in the makeshift shelter. . . . At around noon, our little community split into two. We were part of the "deserters" who went to meet other neighbors. We kept on running, crossing through the fields on the way to Mandeville. Wounded cattle fell nearby. We weren't sure exactly where we were, and a girl had lost her clogs. All of a sudden, we were face to face with Allied tanks. Stunned, they stopped lobbing artillery shells. We had crossed the front—we were with the Americans! After exchanging a few words with the soldiers, they led us to a barn where we could spend the night. They handed out chocolate, cookies, chewing gum and . . . cigarettes![2]

The Fenands were not the last to cross enemy lines. Throughout the summer, civilians found themselves catching their first glimpse of an American in a no-man's-land between two opposing armies. Albert Lehodey of Rémilly accidentally liberated himself with one of his five children, Bernard, when he left a shelter to fix a fence. Unfortunately, he left much of his family behind.

After lunch, I ventured out with my son to the gate at the edge of the field, where a German shell had just landed. What a surprise it was to come across soldiers dressed in khaki, behind a hedge. We couldn't believe our eyes. Our curiosity piqued, we climbed onto the hedge and found ourselves face to face with the men tasked with liberating all of France.

"I'm French," I said. "Are you American soldier?"

"Yes, yes," one of the Yanks replied. "Come with us."

I stole a glance at Bernard. It was tough to take the first step toward the Liberation! But we did, and there we were on the American lines, sitting in a trench, showing the soldiers our papers. We then crossed a field near the town where ten American soldiers had already died for us. Others had just been severely wounded; one was lying in a pool of his own blood and had lost a leg, which we found fifty meters away, hanging from the branch of a tree.[3]

The GIs brought Lehodey and his son back to Lehodey's own house, now transformed into an American headquarters. Lehodey's good English earned him a place in the camp. But he was worried about his wife and his four other children, who were staying at a shelter now in-between enemy lines. Little Bernard could think of nothing else but his mother.

The major subjected me to a grilling in my kitchen. As I spoke some English, we were able to understand each other perfectly and got along well. I gave him information about the Germans' position, told him about my family in Clos Vautier,[4] the number of people remaining in Rémilly, etc. We got along so well that the major wanted us to stay with them until Rémilly was completely liberated. We hadn't been expecting that. I wondered what our family would think.

Bernard seemed dismayed to have to stay in the wide-open building, filled with visions of war and continually bombed by the Nazis. "I want to be with Mother," he said to me softly. "There's nothing we can do," I replied. "If we try to go back toward the Germans, we would be shot on sight. We can't go back to the enemy because of the information I've provided about them. You'll have to make do. The shelling may be rough now, but one day you'll be proud of this adventure and how much it helped toward our liberation."

Bernard came to grips with the situation, especially when the Yanks brought us a slew of food that we hadn't tasted in four years . . . and then the major led us to the precise spot where we were supposed to stay put, thirty meters behind an apple orchard. Using sheet metal and bundles of wood, we built a makeshift shelter against a hedge behind the trees to protect us against errant German shell fire.[5]

Meanwhile, the Germans began shelling the area sheltering the rest of Lehodey's family. Fearful for their lives, his wife and four other children moved to a farm half a kilometer away. When Lehodey woke up the next day, he decided he must let his family know his location, lest they think him dead. He dreamed up a plan to visit, only to find them gone.

I let Bernard in on my scheme and promised to be back in an hour, then left on the byroad toward Clos Vautier. I came across an American patrol led by two officers, who were out in front of the soldiers. I followed the officers, making it seem as if I knew them. I arrived at a little lane where the American advance party had established a position, across from the German front line. Two black soldiers, who were lying low in their hole, warned me that it would be very dangerous to go any farther. I told them that there weren't any Germans there, and that I would be back soon. I soon arrived at the shelter where I thought my family was. It was a horrible letdown to find it empty. I ran across the German lines to the nearby farm, La Halle, where I found everyone who had feared for our lives and shook them awake. I quickly recounted our adventure and encouraged them to join us in our shelter, brandishing a white flag for the journey.

It was a tremendously emotional moment for everyone present. Tears of joy ran down their faces, which looked exhausted after their sleepless night. I threw little American treats onto the straw bed for the children, to show them that I had become American, whereas they were still German. We hugged and parted ways— time was of the essence. I traipsed through the fields of my child-hood, across the German and American lines, arriving at 7:00 a.m. to find Bernard sleeping with clenched fists. When he woke up, I told him about my excursion: "Mother knows we're here; all is well."[6]

The Normans were a stubborn people. Even in the midst of a battle or bombing raid, they insisted that the crops be planted and the cows milked. Many died trying to perform such tasks. In the southern Cotentin, Gustave Marie only reluctantly gave up his chores when he walked out his back door into a battle under way.

On June 15, three Americans who appeared to be on a recon patrol were torn to shreds by mortar fire near the buildings. We knew that the Liberation wasn't far away. Although there was no fighting, we got little sleep that night. I woke up at 6:00 a.m. The cows needed to be milked and couldn't wait any longer. In order to limit the risk, I brought them to the field behind the barn, near the courtyard. I set off on my way with two women helpers so that it wouldn't take as long. We heard the first gunshots just as we arrived in the field. We decided to bring the cows back into the barn as a precaution, but before we could finish, US soldiers arrived from all directions.

Shots were being fired from every which way. Armored vehicles rolled across the field. We decided to forget about the cows and re-turn to the others in the house as quickly as possible. It wasn't to be. We were captured and ushered into the incessant flow of men and vehicles. They led us toward Hameau des Coqs and Lebrun's farm, a few hundred meters away, and left us with the other French. We had no idea what had happened to those left in the house, and they, too, must have been left with a lot of unanswered questions. Were they dead? Were we dead? The battle lasted the entire day;

it was only in the evening that things calmed down. Since none of the soldiers seemed to be watching over us, we decided to return to the house to meet back up with the others. We made our way back though the groups of soldiers, arriving at the house without a hitch.

We were relieved to be back, but nerves were still running high—the day had been a traumatic one. Two groups of families had spent the entire time in separate parts of the house, unable to communicate. The battle was fought in the courtyard. The American infantrymen climbed onto the roof to determine the enemy's location. An American had positioned himself in the doorway of the apartment, five meters across from the house. He was killed by a bullet to the head. Shell casings littered the ground at his feet. He himself had taken a few victims before meeting his end. All the Germans in the field were killed. They had not been able to make it out into the open—most of them died while holed up in their trenches. The Allies had also suffered heavy losses: thirty-some corpses were on the ground near the house. We were surprised to find that one of the dead German soldiers was wearing civilian clothes under his uniform. He had on the wedding suit of one of the men in the house, who lived in a nearby village. The soldier had clearly been waiting for the ideal moment to cut and run.

The bodies of the Allied soldiers were removed the next day, unlike the bodies of the dead Germans, which were left there for quite some time. There was one in front of a door in the courtyard. Although we had to step over him to enter the apartment, we were not inclined to move him. We may have been afraid that he was booby-trapped, but above all, we didn't consider it our business to do so.[7]

Normans treated the bodies of German and Allied soldiers very differently. The German corpses lay exposed, often for days and weeks. Children robbed them of boots and other valuables. Whereas a German body was left faceup and bereft of belongings, an Allied one remained facedown, covered, and most often decorated with a bouquet of flowers.

FROM ONE HELL TO ANOTHER

Most families had no choice but to leave. Bombardment rendered their homes uninhabitable. In addition, the Germans forced the evacuation of many areas so as to maneuver more easily. They also sought to prevent civilians from giving intelligence to the enemy. In these cases, there was no forewarning, plan, or system of assistance. As the battle neared, the Germans would simply knock on doors and order civilians to leave, often under the threat of death.[8]

Normans set out with one of two destinations in mind. First, they tried to move deep into the countryside, where bombing was less frequent. Second, they sought relatives or friends in other regions whose homes (they hoped) were safe. In general, refugees moved south and east. On the way, they built makeshift shelters by digging trenches near hedgerows, then covering these holes with sticks. Still other families huddled in subterranean caves, mines, or church vaults. Refugees usually traveled in groups of twenty to thirty, composed of many families. Constant Allied bombing forced them to interrupt their journey and take cover as best they could, sometimes several times a day.

The primary means of transportation was walking. Most Normans didn't own cars, and even if they did, there was no gasoline. The lucky ones had horse-drawn carts on which to prop the elderly and children. Others loaded up wheelbarrows, baby carriages, and bicycles. Some brought little or nothing, having had only thirty minutes to pack their belongings. Still others brought everything they owned, including mattresses, sheep, cows, and goats. In some towns, refugees received assistance in the form of hot meals or new shoes. Elsewhere, they relied only on the generosity of individuals.

The journey was filled with unexpected dangers. Refugees who lived near the Allied landing areas often came face-to-face with the fighting. Jean Flamand from Sainte-Mère-Église remembers that when he and his family sought to flee the battlefield, they ended up running into it. The Merderet was a north–south river running just west of Sainte-Mère-Église. Taking the bridges that spanned it would allow the Americans to move west and north. Hence the bridge over the Merderet to La Fière was one of the earliest battles fought by the GIs.

On the morning of June 7, during a lull in the fighting, the adults in our group decided it would be best to travel from the stud farm to another farm deep in the countryside, about two or three kilometers away.[9] . . . Little did we know, we were headed straight toward another bridgehead where a fierce battle was under way for control over the bridge to La Fière that spans the Merderet River. The Allies had stepped up the landings on Omaha Beach; taking this bridge was of prime importance. The thirty-two of us left, walking one in front of the other. Leading the group was a stableman holding up a piece of white cloth. We had placed my disabled grandmother as comfortably as possible in a wheelbarrow, which my father was now pushing. . . . Despite being knocked and jostled about in the rudimentary vehicle, she didn't complain one bit, wincing only at times when the wheel fell into a rut.

We would walk a few steps, hear the whistle of an artillery shell, lie down flat on our stomachs, and then get back up, only to repeat the exercise. It was an especially trying ordeal for our grandmother, who was stuck in the wheelchair and couldn't move, as it was for the woman holding a crying infant in her arms, who wanted the milk it had been deprived of for several days because of the horrible war.

We were nearing the end of our journey when a group of paratroopers suddenly emerged from a hedge and surrounded us. One of them rushed toward us and explained through a mix of gestures and a few unintelligible words in French that it would be sheer madness to go any farther. We were close to La Fière Bridge and about three hundred meters from the railroad bridge used by the Paris–Cherbourg train. We had left one hell, only to find ourselves in another. . . . A sergeant named James Blues, who was wearing a khaki wool cap, took hold of the wheelbarrow and led us to a field. The Americans soldiers gave us blankets, milk for the baby, and things to eat and drink. Our grandmother was able to make herself comfortable, lie down, and finally get some rest.

We stayed there for two days and two nights. An American soldier kept watch over us the whole time and chatted with us in German. Gliders dotted the surrounding fields. Some were intact, but most were broken or in shreds. There were paratroopers hanging in the trees who had been there since June 5. . . . A bit farther away, the battle for La Fière Bridge—where James Blues fought—was raging. We could hear the sound of the machine guns and a whistling noise in the leaves that would make us huddle close together down in our trench. We didn't dare go outside.

Two dramatic events occurred during these two rough days. First, we saw our sentry abruptly take a knee, shoulder his rifle, aim, and fire two shots. He stood up, went into the field, came back, and said, "Deutch [sic] kaput zwei."[10] He had just killed two Germans who had ventured onto the path that ran along the field toward La Fière Bridge. The American had saved us again.

Second, a violent explosion behind our hedge sent us flying to the ground, and we were hit by shrapnel. I had a minor injury to my left leg. My mother felt a hard object hit her in the back. It was a piece of shrapnel. She picked it up and then quickly dropped it, because it was burning hot. A shell had landed behind us, in the area where we had originally planned to stay. Yet again, the Americans had saved us.

They rightly thought that we were too close to the road, so they led us to where we were when the shell hit, which they believed would be safer. The battle of La Fière Bridge ended on the third day. Our friends left us, which meant that we no longer had any protection. Our parents decided to go to the nearest village, Vaulaville, where we could stay with people we knew. When we . . . arrived in the village, we found that it was safely in the hands of the Americans, who were speaking with the locals. The fighting was over: peace at last.[11]

As Flamand's memoir suggests, the GIs did what they could to keep civilians out of harm's way. His family ultimately found refuge with friends in nearby Vaulaville, west of Sainte-Mère-Église. Odette Eudes, also of Sainte-Mère-Église, tells a similar story of being caught in the battle at La Fière. At first, Eudes, her family, and her neighbors tried to hide from the fighting in a cellar. Then they decided to leave, brandishing a makeshift white flag. Like Flamand's grandmother, the elderly woman in Eudes's group had to make do with a wheelbarrow for a seat.

The fighting resumed during the night. The Germans came back determined to take Sainte-Mère, and we found ourselves right in the cross fire. Our house had one window and two glass doors facing each other. There was a closet near the front door hidden by a curtain. When we went to get our clothes later, they all had bullet holes. It was beyond belief.

That night, the stable doors had come open, and Monsieur Levesque, who could see the stable from the cellar where he was hiding, yelled to Papa to go and close them. Papa ran out to close the door, and on his way back, he spotted a soldier sitting atop a wall about two meters high. Once the cellar door was closed, the soldier shot a bullet through it, which landed in the wall, ten centimeters from my brother Jean's head. Adding to our fears, the mare's stable caught fire, and the flames spread to the hay where we were lying and began to burn.

Monsieur Levesque called Papa a second time to open the door for the poor mare, which was whinnying with fear, but Papa and Monsieur Rioult were too busy putting out the hay fire. Sadly, the poor animal perished in the flames, but we were fortunate enough to succeed in extinguishing our fire.

Our stomachs were still tied in knots as we huddled in a corner of the cellar. We stayed there until 10:00 a.m., when we decided to venture out, as there was no end to the fighting in sight. Along with all the neighbors, an Alsatian couple, and some others (there were thirty-two people in all), we formed a group in Madame Jouan's kitchen. Also with us was Madame Jouan's mother, who was eighty years old and had just undergone surgery. She was lying in a wheelbarrow, waiting for us to leave. Monsieur Rioult was to lead us out. He had told us not to stand in front of the fireplace, which later collapsed.

We prepared ourselves to go three times. Each time, he [Monsieur Rioult] opened the door, then closed it. On our fourth try, we made it out. We left in single file, with Monsieur and Madame Philippe (the Alsatians) walking in front, carrying a white handkerchief tied to a stick. We each had a bundle to carry: a sack of flour, covers, bread and a bit of food, etc. We took the path toward La Fière, and all along the way, there were soldiers in foxholes, in shooting position. But the unfortunate souls who had come for us were all dead. It nevertheless felt like they would turn around and start shooting at us.

Deep into the path, we entered a large field. When we were about halfway across it, a bullet whizzed past Monsieur Levesque and me, giving us yet another fright. When we reached the American Red Cross, Monsieur and Madame Benoit stayed behind; a few hours later, Madame Benoit gave birth to a baby girl. The Americans led us to a large tunnel-like ditch where we could lie down. It was a place they themselves had stayed. We spent three days and three nights there.[12]

Juliette Brault's family also spent several nights sleeping in fields, surrounded on all sides by the war. Like Flamand's family, hers came from Sainte-Mère-Église and found refuge in Vaulaville. Like countless other Normans, she was separated from a loved one, her fiancé, with only rumors for information.

Some people fell ill due to the violence of the bombings, while others became completely motionless. We also heard screaming and learned, in the midst of the panic, that civilians had lost their lives. Immediately thereafter, the decision was made to flee, and we had to leave Sainte-Mère-Église as quickly as possible and reach the fields. It was pandemonium. There was no time to weigh ourselves down with unnecessary belongings—we didn't even have time to take our clothes and food.

After wandering about for a moment, we finally found one another in the fields. Among the twenty-nine of us was a heavily pregnant woman named Madame Marcel Marie. We slept in ditches for three nights, in makeshift shelters. We had to be careful, because the fighting was raging all around us and the Germans weren't far! We found ourselves in the heat of the battle—shots were coming from all directions! The Germans held their ground and remained on part of the land. The Americans were in front of us, and up above, planes were flying nap-of-the-earth, making such deafening noise that we thought they were going to crash down on us. My little brother, Michel, was very scared and cried nonstop. We were all afraid, hiding like hunted animals, with no idea what to do or where to go.

I was worried and thinking about my fiancé, Georges, whom I hadn't had any news from since June 6. What had happened to him?

Then, on June 9, we left the ditch where we had taken refuge. We hadn't eaten for practically three days, and hunger had tied our stomachs in knots. We traveled to Vaulaville, a kilometer west of Sainte-Mère-Église, and stopped at a farm run by a very welcoming couple, Monsieur and Madame Fortier. Thirty or so tired, scared refugees were there. Eating was no longer a concern. There was milk, eggs, and poultry. The farmers killed a calf to ease our pain. Later, four men decided to head into town to find flour, meat, and bread—all of which were sorely needed. My father, my brother Maurice, Monsieur Legoupillot, and Monsieur Lefrance went into the village and returned fairly quickly. They said that Sainte-Mère-Église was unrecognizable: most of the shops had been destroyed, and the streets were strewn with rubble and slate roof tiles. Danger was everywhere!

They told us that we had to be very careful to prevent hurting ourselves. The next day, I decided with a friend, Mademoiselle Jeanne Legoupillot (Pentecôte), to go into town. We were shaking in our boots! In rue Cap de Laine, there was a *vachère*, a horse-drawn cart usually used to transport animals. We took a look inside out of curiosity, and what we saw was ghastly: it was full of German corpses. On the way back, two German planes flew low overhead, targeted us, and began firing! We first flung ourselves against the wall of a girls' school for protection, then dove into a ditch full of stinging nettles! We were scratching ourselves all day long. We were told that the fighting was fierce in Montebourg, and that the town had been taken, then lost. It was said to be horrendous there—nasty, bloody hand-to-hand combat and dead soldiers everywhere! In Fresville, my fiancé's village, the local population was forced to flee, and some people took refuge under the second bridge in a washhouse. I remained hopeful that Georges was safe and sound. Then one day I heard a rumor that their hiding spot had been bombed, and everyone hiding there had been killed.[13]

Just south of Sainte-Mère-Église, still another Norman and his family were trying to escape the shelling of the first hours of the campaign. They, too, were witness to some of the first American casualties. The bodies of Americans evoked gratitude in French civilians, who saw in them the realization of the war's highest ideals.

That evening, the BBC announced that the Americans had taken Carentan. The euphoria was short-lived, however, because an hour after the small group of Americans had left, a barrage of shells landed around the farm. We would have to cross a field and follow a covered path for a few hundred meters to reach the road to Périers and head down the hill.

Taking advantage of a lull, we left the farm and placed our belongings on the trailer. We stayed tightly grouped, pushing the trailer forward but making sure not to run. We made it safely across the open field, after what seemed like an eternity! At the entrance to the path, I nearly stepped on an American soldier lying prone at the edge, his gun pointed in our direction. He wasn't alone—on either side were other prone soldiers, weapons unlimbered and ready to shoot. They let us pass, and we continued to a road with an anti-tank gun in position to fire. Other soldiers were lying down or sitting in ditches. One was stretched out on the ground and covered with a tent canvas. I will never forget seeing this soldier who died for us, who had come on our soil, in Normandy, to fight for the lives of others and paid for it with his life.[14]

Still other refugees had to deal with German soldiers. Thirteen-year-old Daniel Fossey and his family found refuge in a house in Beslon, at the base of the Cotentin Peninsula. All went well until the 2nd SS Panzer Division ("Das Reich") arrived, the same soldiers who had committed atrocities in Oradour-sur-Glâne some weeks before. In that small Limousin village, "Das Reich" had murdered 642 civilians, shooting the men and burning the women and children. Evicted by these men, the Fossey group sought shelter in a field, then awoke to realize that the war was following them.

We found shelter for the horses and cows, and scythed grass for them. The first night was relatively calm and restful. The next day, we made plans, and my parents seemed set on staying there as long as possible. Sadly, our respite was short-lived. Germans arrived in the village in late July. What misfortune! They were particularly nervous, arrogant SS men. I remember reading "DAS REICH" and "DER FÜHRER" on the sleeves of their jackets. They parked their vehicles under the apple trees and entered the houses and outbuildings. Madame Martin, whose upbringing and sense of propriety couldn't have been further from that of the SS men, tried to reason with them in an attempt to preserve the intimacy of her humble abode. At first, the Germans didn't reply. They walked in without paying us any attention; then one of them, an officer, I believe, turned to face us and pointed to the door with a stern "Heraus!" followed by "Civils Heraus!" Stunned, Madame Martin asked Papa what he had said, and Papa replied, "It's easy to understand—he's kicking us out, and now isn't the time for discussion." At the time, we had no idea what had happened at Oradour-sur-Glâne, where this command—for they were the perpetrators—had massacred the local population. We had no choice but to comply, so we took refuge in the barn.

Under Papa's guidance, we decided to build a shelter. Soon all the men were working away in a corner of the field, under the trees, where we built a trench big enough to hold fifteen to twenty people. We covered the top with logs provided by Monsieur Loslier, then bundles of sticks, and camouflaged it all with branches. The front was drawing closer, and we could hear artillery fire. The roof of the barn wasn't much of a roof at all, so we decided to spend our first night in the trench. There was no thought of lying down—we wrapped ourselves in blankets and sat huddled together. As if our luck couldn't get any worse, that night, or perhaps the night after, we were awakened by guttural German voices and the noise of their trucks. What were they doing? They were right next to us. Papa peeked outside and saw them setting up guns in a nearby field on the other side of the hedge. The din had only just begun—they fired endless volleys. Sleep was out of the question, and life was a nightmare. Everyone was afraid that the Americans would locate the battery, and we'd be forced to pick up and run.

During the night of August 2, I fell into a deep sleep and Papa woke me up, because the shooting had stopped. He went out to see what was going on and came back after inspecting the area, proclaiming, "The artillery is gone, as are the Germans." It was great news, but how long would it last? I forgot to mention that the day before we had seen our first jeep, with its big white star on the hood, but it was driven by an SS man. In the field near Monsieur Loslier's house, several Germans were examining it with a curiosity equal to our own. One of them tested out the machine gun, shooting rounds into the ground. As this was happening, we heard a distinctive whistling sound and then an explosion, which snapped us back to reality. A shell landed near us, and others followed. I took to my heels and went back into the trench.

On August 3, 1944, at dawn, we heard a steady rumble of artillery explosions over by the main road. It was barely daybreak, but André was resolute: "I'm going to find the Americans." He headed out with Yves Martin through the fields toward Gros Caillou junction. As it turned out, they didn't have to look very far. It still wasn't very bright out, so when they saw silhouettes of men snaking in and out of a hedge, they weren't sure whether they were Germans or Allies. Moving in to get a closer look, they were soon stopped by the men and found themselves face to face with Americans. Fortunately, André spoke English, and told them that there weren't any more Germans in the village. After what seemed like an eternity, André and Yves Martin came back, shouting, "They're here! They're here!" And indeed, there were the Americans, marching in single file and still on the lookout, as I stood there wide-eyed.[15]

THE CRIES OF CHILDREN

Normandy that summer was no place for children. In her diary of June 8, fourteen-year-old Christine Fenand describes the horror of the war in Trévières for the smallest Normans.

> The sound of gunfire drew close, and shells whistled above our heads. "That one wasn't far off," my brother said. "The second one landed closer, and the third will hit us." He was right. The third exploded on a tree at the end of the ditch. The shrapnel killed my 23-year-old brother and fatally wounded four members of the same family, aged 9, 10, 15, and 16! . . . The cries of the wounded sent everyone running for their lives. Unaware of the extent of the damage, we fled, stepping over the splayed bodies and ignoring the parents' cries. The smoke and smell of burning were unbearable. We followed a small wounded child, who cried while escaping: "It's burning me! It's burning me!" In attempting to jump over a fence, she fell, exhausted, into the arms of a gentleman who managed to catch her. She would be cared for by the English in Bayeux, but would die on the operating table; both her arm and her intestines were perforated. She and her brother, who was also killed, had been sent to Trévières by their parents in Le Havre in order to keep them safe.[16]

Newborn babies were particularly vulnerable. The dust, dirt, noise, and lack of food, including breast milk, all took their toll on the tiniest Normans. In the chaos of the invasion, Gustave Marie lost his infant daughter.

> The Germans were very nervous. They came into the house and demanded that we leave immediately: "Very dangerous, Tommies soon here!" My wife had given birth two days earlier. I explained that it would be impossible for us to leave. Observing that she had indeed just given birth, they gave in and didn't kick us out. We grew

increasingly worried. We decided to baptize the baby. I headed out into the fields to find the Abbé of Brix, who had fled to a neighboring village. The priest was petrified and refused to make the journey. He instructed me on what to do and say to baptize the child. In the end, a woman staying in the house baptized my baby girl. It was impossible for the baby to live under those conditions. She died several days later due to lack of treatment. In a nearby village, another child died several weeks later under the exact same circumstances.[17]

Witnessing the wounding of children was particularly difficult for Normans. Of the fierce fighting west of Saint-Lô in mid-July, Arsène Quinette remembers most vividly the cries of injured children whose parents had been killed in the battle.

On Monday, July 17, at 10:00 a.m., three American tanks advanced slowly toward Lozon, shooting up the dense hedges with all their firepower. Through the smoke of the battle, we could see their flags flying atop the antennas. Bullets crashed into and ricocheted off the walls of the farm, and cracked the tiles of the roof. . . .

During the afternoon, German bullets whizzed and whistled around the house. We stayed inside. It was a wise decision: a German mortar round exploded right in the middle of our empty courtyard. That was when the first American soldiers arrived. At their request, I led them around the farm's outbuildings—cellars, stables, barns, hangars, and granaries—so they could make sure there weren't any German soldiers hiding there. Everyone was wondering the same thing: How far had the Allied tanks gotten? Had they reached the road from Saint-Lô to Périers, as everyone was hoping? . . .

Once the danger had subsided, we were preparing to take to the road again when we heard someone crying in Albert Palla's house. Monsieur Courtel crossed the courtyard, entered the house, then reappeared on the doorstep and called out to us.

We knew from the tone of his voice that something was amiss. We went into the kitchen, which had been destroyed by a shell that must have entered through the window. Despite the dwindling sunlight, we discovered three of their children near the chimney, at the entrance to the woodshed. There were two girls, who appeared to be unharmed, and a little boy, who was about three years old, with a fractured arm that hung lifelessly.

We were horrified by this discovery. The children were traumatized both physically and mentally, disfigured by a mask of dust with a tunnel of tears, their eyes glazed over with terror. The sight of the three civilian victims and these three little orphans was a plea for peace that impressed on us the true horror of war, often the result of the mad ambition of some men.

We brought the three children into my parents' house, taking turns carrying the injured little boy, whose arm hurt so bad that he couldn't help but complain. Madame Novince, Madame Courtel, and my mother rushed to the children. Bowls of milk were soon on the table. The injured boy stopped crying and pleaded, "Give me something to drink!" He drank the first cup of milk in a single gulp, then a second, then a third. "More, more!" he continued, drinking a fourth cup and maybe even a fifth; I can't remember. I had never in my life seen such a thirsty child.

The women began to treat the injured boy by candlelight. They cut off the sleeves of his clothes, but despite their bravery, they were overwhelmed by the severity of the wound. They managed to clean the edge of the cut, wrap the little arm in a bandage, and set it using a small board.

In the middle of the night, we were sleeping fully dressed in the cellar when we were awakened by a large explosion. My father and I jumped to our feet and cracked the door open. We were besieged by an acrid, irritating odor, and the courtyard was illuminated by a sparkling, phosphorescent glow: a German phosphorescent round had hit one of the main buildings and exploded. We were lucky that a fire didn't break out, because animal feed was stored in the building.

That same morning, on July 18, my father left for town at dawn. First he went to see Dr. Lepage, who, because he had lost everything, advised my father to go to the American Red Cross to have the young Lair boy treated. His next stop was at the residence of Marie Maudouin, the grandmother of the Lair children, to inform her of the tragic turn of events. Alas, she had already been evacuated.

Later, Monsieur Novince and Monsieur Courtel went to the US aid station. They were forced to crawl along the hedges a number of times along the way due to exploding shells, particularly near Le Lieu Acher. They came back home soon thereafter in a jeep, with two Americans. One of them, a medic, took possession of the child and said he would be transported to Carentan. We had just enough time before the jeep pulled off to pin a card to his shirt with his name. We later learned that little Gérard Lair had to have his arm amputated.[18]

The presence of death throughout Normandy was traumatic for everyone, but particularly for children. Young Christian Letourneur remembers the dead south of Sainte-Mère-Église shortly after D-Day.

Another painful memory remains present in my mind. A few days after the sixth of June, hundreds of dead American soldiers lay in rows on a plot of land in Carquebut that was the site of the first American cemetery. As I was an altar boy, the parish priest of Blosville and Houerville at the time, Father Paul Lejard, requested my aid to give the absolution of the dead. An American chaplain accompanied the priest, and although they didn't speak each other's language, the two were able to converse in Latin. We strode past row after row of dead soldiers. Never before had a field seemed so large; it was very hard to bear—all I wanted to do was to leave![19]

WITNESSING THE WAR

Normans came to know the misery of war. They watched as the Allies were taken away on stretchers, chests torn by shrapnel and jaws clenched in pain. They saw men exhausted beyond measure or half-crazy from combat. And they were with soldiers in the hour of their death. This was the case from the very first night of the invasion, when Désiré Pottier observed the killing of Americans taken prisoner by the Germans.

> That same morning, we were shaken by some awful news, which became even more dreadful when we saw it with our own eyes that afternoon with Bernard Leinot. On the night of June 5–6, a group of paratroopers descended into the Cotentin Peninsula, but they did not all land in the same area as had been planned. Many touched down so far from the landing area that they were taken prisoner by the Germans, who loaded them on trucks and formed a convoy on the road from Périers to Saint-Lô. US aircraft spotted the trucks filled with soldiers and enfiladed them with machine gun fire, thinking they had annihilated the Germans, while in reality they had unwittingly killed their own soldiers. The burned remnants of the trucks were still smoking when we came across them, as were their grisly contents. From Les Pins junction to Le Mesnil Vigot, we came across the charred remains of young soldiers who were about our age and had met a tragic end. . . . If their poor parents knew how they had died . . .[20]

Sometimes there was little Normans could do except offer a gift of *calva*. After the battle at La Fière on June 7, Jean Flamand witnessed a traumatized American soldier.

> Finally at rest, the soldiers were the survivors of La Fière Bridge, as their tired, dirty faces and torn clothes attested. One wild-eyed sol-

dier stared blankly into the distance, holding an unpinned grenade closely to his chest. An officer was reasoning with him. He looked completely shattered! Did he want to commit suicide? He must have gone through some ghastly things during the fighting. One of the locals came up to the soldier with a bottle of Calvados and offered it to him. He soon calmed down, and his face became less tense. He took the bottle, at which point the officer deftly grabbed the grenade. The officer and the villager had just saved his life, as well as those of the people who had been watching the scene unfold from a distance.

We later found out that the heroic soldier had seen his three best friends die before his eyes, killed by German bullets. It had driven him to the brink. As he was taken away in a jeep, I saw village onlookers wiping away tears. This tragic incident haunted me for a long time—I can still picture him, shocked and wild-eyed. I think I could still recognize him, this battle-worn soldier.[21]

Marcel Leveel's family, who lived just south of the landing beaches, tried to make friends with another traumatized soldier, who had taken up residence in a field near their house.

An American had stayed back alone in the abandoned camp. When I had a look in the fields, I didn't see him, but the next day he briefly appeared at Chan's house looking for something to drink. He gradually gathered the courage to eat with us. We didn't pay special attention to him. . . . The thing he did most often was sleep. If we wanted to see him, we would call him and he'd come. He was very calm, shy even, pudgy, and very fair-haired—he looked like the Cadum baby.[22] He was very fond of cider, but didn't stay with us for very long.

One afternoon, on my way out of the house, I heard high-pitched cries coming from the field. It was a rabbit. I went to the cages, and the soldier was there. He had opened one and was holding the animal by its ears. He tried to make it lie down by pulling on its rear paws. He was giddy and giggled. I had no trouble reasoning with him and getting him to put the rabbit back in its place. He was completely drunk and could barely stand up. Without a word, apart from his giggling, he gave me a big wave and teetered back to his field. He stayed there for five or six days, then a jeep with two MPs arrived at Chan's place and took him away.[23]

All Normans, even children, were privy to the terrible effects of war on the human body. Désiré Pottier remembers one particularly gruesome scene in the battle among the hedgerows.

They went a couple of meters farther—ten at most—and arrived at the hedge, in the street behind the hedge where the Germans were lying in wait. Then the gunfight began. It was painful to listen to the war cries of the soldiers charging with their bayonets. The two tanks began firing shot after shot from the positions described above. I gathered that they were shooting at the Germans who were threatening to flank the small group of Americans that had ventured a tad too far in front of the Vignettes buildings. The bullets whistled past, landing in the earthen wall of the façade. The entire exchange of gun and cannon fire lasted an hour and five minutes. Then it all suddenly stopped, as if a single man were commanding the two antagonists. The "Yanks" brought back their wounded; those with only slight injuries were laid on stretchers in the courtyard. The severely wounded—twenty-one to twenty-four of the men were in very bad shape—were placed on blankets in the two houses. Some were still taking drags from a cigarette despite it all. Severed arms, bits of lung sticking out of rib cages . . . it was almost unbearable. The young children watched unflinchingly at a sight that forty-five of the forty-eight civilians present had never witnessed. It was astonishing to see all these people who, no matter what they came up against, seemed unfazed by this harrowing situation.[24]

SHELTERING THE WOUNDED

As best they could, Normans aided the wounded. Often at the risk of their own lives, they offered shelter, brandy, and food as well as transport to first-aid stations. In Montebourg, north of Sainte-Mère-Église, the Germans launched a determined counterattack on June 7. There Maurice Allix was witness to their ambush of Americans. The Nazis hid behind a long wall bordering the road into town. They allowed the GIs to advance up this road, then picked them off with sniper fire. Hiding in a cellar at the house of the Guyonnet brothers, Allix and other civilians watched the drama unfold. Allix tells the story.

> There were a lot of wounded. One American, a lieutenant, took a bullet on the walkway at the Guyonnets' house. After a while, once the attack had ended, we heard him wailing in agony. The boys came up from the cellar. It still wasn't safe to go out, so they waited. When they were able to get to him, they dragged him out and took him with us. . . . He had been pierced by a bullet—it had cut through him like a knife. You could see the tendons in his neck . . . everything was exposed . . . you could even see his carotid artery. He was a lucky man: the shot had basically peeled back his skin.[25]

Despite the severity of his wound, the lieutenant remained conscious while Charline Genu gave him some Calvados—the only "medicine" available. Allix remembers how disciplined the soldier remained.

> He kept his big Parabellum tucked against his stomach and wouldn't let go of it for anything. Down in the cellar, we were worried that if some Germans came in, he would shoot! He didn't speak a word of French. Charline Genu, who spoke English, tried

several times to explain the situation, but he refused to let go of his weapon.

Then the worst happened. Some Germans came down to see if the civilians were harboring any Americans. The Normans were able to roll the lieutenant up in an old blanket and hide him while the Germans scanned the crowd. Unable to find anything, they left. But no sooner did they depart than—equally dangerous—the Americans came.

> That evening or the next day, when they saw that the first patrol they'd sent had been decimated (I believe there was only one sur-vivor: the wounded soldier who was with us), another American patrol arrived via Highway 13 to "clean up" the area by throwing grenades into the houses. They must have heard noise in the cellar. We went upstairs just in time to prevent the guy from throwing a grenade into the crowd of fifty or sixty people who were there.

Despite their broken English, the Guyonnet brothers were able to explain the situation to the GIs. Two of them opened the cellar door, and the wounded lieutenant called out to a voice he recog-nized. The GIs were reunited and the civilians saved.[26]

Normans could only do so much. Yet besides offering *calva*, they saved lives by bringing the wounded soldiers to safety in their back-yards. Refugee Michel Braley tells his diary how he and his family tried to help two wounded soldiers on the day of his liberation.

> [American] soldiers continued to arrive, but the German artillery was still firing, and we were basically confined to our home. The shells were still falling fairly close to us, and a steady stream of ma-chine gun fire soon followed. We didn't even think to eat. A succes-sion of shells thundered down around the house; it was impossible

to tell whether they were German or American. The courtyard was full of shrapnel. A dozen shells landed in a field thirty meters from us; the situation was tense. The Americans were advancing, but the Germans were lying in ambush in the trees and could pick off their enemies. We caught sight of a wounded American soldier walking toward the farm. He came in, had a rest, and gestured that he was thirsty. We gave him coffee with brandy. His hand was wounded. Papa was able to understand a few sentences he wrote on a scrap of paper: he wanted to go to the aid station, one hundred meters from the house. We showed him which way to go. Before he left, he took out his New Testament and a photo of his parents. We told him that we were Protestant also. He thanked us and left. The shells continued to rain down. An hour later, we thought we heard shouting, but didn't pay any attention to it. Then we heard someone shout, "French! French!" Papa understood that it was a soldier that needed help, so he went out to find him. A bullet had gone through the American's foot, and he could hardly move. We brought him into the house and, after giving him a drink, we took him to the aid station, at about six o'clock in the morning.[27]

FROM BATTLEFIELDS TO MINEFIELDS

As the Germans retreated, they covered their path with mines, trip wires, and booby traps. In the days and weeks after liberation, accidents were common. Farmers and fishermen ran into mines in the course of their labor; children tragically mistook grenades and mortar bombs for toys. Raymond Avignon's memoir demonstrates just how impossible it was for Normans to escape the war even after the battle had passed them by. He remembers seeing the GIs try to de-mine a field in the lower Cotentin. De-mining became a priority among Allied military officials trying to reestablish order in liberated areas.

Equipped with a "frying pan," a sort of metallic dish with a long handle, they checked the road and ditches. We were truly in a minefield. They motioned to us not to advance any farther, so we took the path that led back to the farm. One of us stopped abruptly and pointed at a thin wire laid across the path at about five centimeters from the ground. We stepped over the wire as cautiously as possible, taking great care not to brush against it. The American soldiers must have found a string of mines hidden on either side of the path. And to think that we all made it past without triggering the trip wire! That's what I call getting lucky!

There was a tank sitting in the intersection that had hit a mine. A wounded soldier was brought on a stretcher into the courtyard of the farm. The war was over for him: his left leg was hanging on by a thread of flesh. He refused the glass of Calvados that the farmer tried to give him, but accepted a cigarette from one of his brothers in arms. The small garden in front of the farm had been checked by US de-miners, so my sister and I went to pick up the German helmet that had been forgotten on top of the hedge, but a soldier motioned us to stop. After carefully setting down the helmet, he carefully examined the inside of the hedge. He showed us a thin wire running from the helmet into the bush. A mine was surely tucked away down there. Yet again, luck was definitely on our side. The reason we had to stay in the house the night before became clear. The Germans had laid mines everywhere to protect their retreat. The owner of the farm, who had lent us his barn, was absolutely intent on milking his cows. It was an unfortunate move, for a few hours later, we had to recover his mine-shredded body from a hunting ground leading to the field. Needless to say, the scene that followed the poor man's return was painful.[28]

The deadly helmet was a common thing. Knowing how much the Allies loved German paraphernalia, the Nazis frequently left helmets and guns behind—rigged with explosives. According to Georgette Leduc, even cooking could get complicated.

> I fled to Mother's house with my six children and my grandmother, who followed us. We had to be careful where we walked, so as not to trip over the electric wires that were strewn about. We arrived to find forty-five refugees, including our parish priest, as well as five German soldiers who had infiltrated the area and were giving themselves up. On July 16, the Americans liberated us at last and visited the houses. We handed over the five Germans, who were surely executed on the spot.
>
> During their short stay, the five soldiers had placed a grenade in the fireplace, rigged with a nearly invisible wire. The Americans noticed it straightaway and warned us not to touch it. It was finally removed six months later! One Sunday, a refugee wanted to put her stew in the laundry room. When she went to fan the fire, she saw that an artillery shell had fallen down the chimney into her stew.[29]

COURAGE! VIVE LA FRANCE!

At the end of July, the American First Army broke out of hedgerow country and began moving south and east toward Rennes. At the same time, General Patton and the newly formed US Third Army moved west to storm Brittany. Patton's goal was to free Breton ports—St.-Malo, St.-Nazaire, Lorient, Brest, and Quiberon Bay—to provide Allied supply posts.

Brittany was a center of the French Resistance, boasting a network of tens of thousands of these fighters. Unified under the aegis of the FFI, or French Forces of the Interior, Resistance groups fought the Germans from the first minutes of the invasion. Their covert actions in the hours before the landings—blowing up railways and bridges, slowing and even stopping German troop movements—were critical to the success of the invasion. By the time Patton moved into Brittany in early August, resisters there had been battling the Germans for weeks. Under Patton's command, these fighters secured bridges, protected the railway along the north coast, and cleared areas of snipers so that US troops could move forward.[30]

The Breton farmer Jean Abily, who tells the story below, joined the Resistance in April 1944 after doing compulsory manual labor for the Germans. Once in the Resistance, he was forced into hiding and put in charge of monitoring German troop movements on Breton rail lines. When an American plane crashed near his village, he seized the aircraft's papers and set out to deliver them to his local FFI network. He did not count on running into four Germans.

I rushed to the scene to find a single-engine aircraft without any weaponry. Despite the heavy damage to the engine, the pilot had deftly performed an impeccable landing on the makeshift "landing strip." This pretty white bird marked no. 298992 V. 95 would never spread its wings again. I quickly grabbed the aircraft's papers from the cockpit. Had they fallen into enemy hands, the documents would have been looked over with a fine-toothed comb. And the enemy was close by. I went back to my house and carefully hid the documents, then went to search for the missing pilot in the woods nearby. I had found out that there was only one man on board when the plane touched down—the second had jumped out with a parachute. Later, I learned that he had been picked up by some Guipavas Resistance fighters and hidden at the Gendarmerie[31] for two days. I was unable to locate the pilot, much to my disappointment. I wanted nothing more than to provide him help and assistance. I couldn't keep the papers from the crashed plane for too long. A brave yet stupid idea crossed my mind: I decided to bring the papers to my commanding officer in the Guipavas Resistance group. I got on my bicycle and started pedaling toward Guipavas. You can only imagine how surprised I was to see four enemy soldiers about sixty meters from Guipavas town hall. In an instant, I became keenly aware of the risk I was running by carrying the compromising documents.

I got off my bicycle and tried to turn around, but one of the Germans cried out, "This way, mister!" It was too late to ditch the papers—they would have noticed. So I continued toward them, assuming a manner "without fear and without reproach." When I was a few steps away from the soldiers, one of them yelled, "Halt!" I stopped like a real soldier. They soon had me surrounded. One took me by the hand while the other took out a pistol. In a haughty tone, they asked me where I was going. I told them that my elderly father was sick, and that I was going to fetch the doctor. This was met with laughter. They said they were going to search me. I politely replied that I didn't see any problem with that. I remained expressionless before my judges, but needless to say, I was gripped by one emotion in particular. I thought my final hour had come. One of them put his hand on the pocket where the precious papers were hidden and asked, "What do you have there?" "My identity papers and my wallet," I replied. Continuing with his investigation, the soldier took off my beret and removed my suspenders. And as a finale, he patted down my shirt and untucked my shirttails to mock and deride me.

I was the only civilian in sight, and all the houses' doors and shutters were closed. During their search, it was very likely that prying eyes watched the little scene unfold. That was of no matter to me. But it didn't stop there. Next, I was subjected to a kind of interrogation to which I was not accustomed. The soldiers asked me a plethora of questions on all sorts of topics. They would often ask four questions at once in an attempt to trip me up.

"You say that you're going to get the doctor! So who at your house is sick?"

"I already told you, it's my father."

"What's wrong with him?"

"His head hurts."

"What did he do today?"

"Harvest crops."

"How old is he?"

"Seventy-two."

"Don't you find it strange that he worked during the day, then got sick in the evening? Do you think the doctor will come to your house?"

"I don't see why he wouldn't."

"So you're not sure as of now?"

"No."

"Where did you arrive from?"

"My house."

"Where do you live?"

"In Kergavarec."

"How far away is your house?"

"About five kilometers."

As soon as they asked this, one of them took out a map of the region and spread it across the hood of their automobile. "What villages are nearby yours?" I gave them the names of several villages, but strangely, my village didn't appear to be marked on the map. "Can you show us where it is?" I told them I'd be happy to. It was decidedly not my day. Things quickly went from bad to worse, as it was confirmed that Kergavarec was not on the map. This provoked an animated conversation among the Krauts, who began acting very aggressively toward me. The one who had me by the hand took one of my fingers and twisted it. I almost cried out in pain, but managed to keep my nerve despite the crazy looks they were shooting me.

"What you just said is a lie; you're not going to fetch the doctor this late in the evening. If we have one shred of evidence that you've made a false statement, you'll be executed immediately."

"My statement was the honest truth, gentlemen."

"Then why isn't your village on the map?"

"I'm not sure, it might be a mistake."

I showed them my identity card, which bore the name of the impossible-to-find village.

"There is no proof that your card isn't a fake. How did you spend your day?"

"Cutting wheat."

"What time did you leave the house? Did you notice anything in particular along the way?"

I answered their questions without appearing the least bit shaken.

"You have a nice bicycle, mister. What do you use it for?"

I thought they were going to steal my bicycle, but they didn't. . . .

"So do you think the doctor will go to your place now?"

"Yes, I think so."

"Well, that's too bad; we forbid you from going to get him. What are you going to do with your so-called sick father?"

"May I please go to the pharmacy and buy some medicine?"

"Do you want to see the doctor for a sick person or for someone who is wounded?"

"I already told you, it's for my father, who is ill."

"Did you see an aircraft hit by German anti-aircraft fire land near St. Divy?"

"I'm sorry, gentlemen, I don't have any information about that. I was very busy taking care of a sick animal during the evening. I can tell you that the children at the farm heard a strange noise coming from an airplane."

Thankfully, the Lord in all his goodness had not endowed these four *Feldengendarmerie* with the requisite intelligence. The questioning drew to a close, and the men conferred with one another in German for a long time. "Listen, mister," one said. "We'll give you five minutes to make a trip to the pharmacy. If, between the fifth and sixth minute, you haven't returned, we'll execute you in front of town hall." My four questioners shared what had transpired with the other soldiers posted along the wall that enclosed the fairgrounds. Machine guns and submachine guns were at the ready, but I was nonetheless given permission to continue on my way—and to tuck in my shirttails. I jumped on my bicycle faster than you can say it. . . .

It was impossible to stray from the road that led to the pharmacy, and equally impossible to deliver the invaluable documents to my officer. I rushed to the pharmacy as quickly as possible. Everything was closed, so I knocked hard on the door. Mademoiselle Poulizac came to the window, stunned. "What do you want?" she asked. "Come down here quickly," I replied. "I have an important mission to carry out." Without hesitation, she opened the door, and I recounted my adventure: I wanted to deliver the papers from the US aircraft that had landed near my house to a trusted individual, but had been a victim of circumstance. Mademoiselle Poulizac agreed to keep the papers in her possession. "Give me a tube of aspirin," I told her, "so I'll be covered if they decide to resume the questioning on the way back." As it turned out, I was stopped again. The four *Feldengendarmerie*, still in position, asked me to show them my medicine. I pulled out the famous tube of aspirin, which may have been my savior. It was 10:00 p.m., a time when the town of Guipavas would normally be gay and lively, but a deathly silence filled the air. The Germans alone were the masters, but their reign would be short-lived—they left that same night, never to come back again.[32]

Abily's story suggests the risks taken by Resistance fighters to secure information and hide pilots. As the Germans became more desperate, their reprisals for such activities became both more frequent and more violent. That summer, Brittany saw two massacres of civilians in the Brest region alone.[33]

At about the same time that Jean Abily was trying to remain calm in the face of his interrogators, a Breton mother received this letter from her son:

Maquis, 8.27.44[34]
Dear Mother,

Thank you for your letter, which I very much enjoyed. Please also send my thanks to Annick for the pack of cigarettes.

Mother, your letter arrived too late—I've already been enlisted in the French Forces of the Interior for a week. I pay a visit to Madame C. from time to time, and she's been very nice to me.

You are the only person that knows I've joined the Resistance, Mother. No need to be ashamed of me anymore. I'll be a good patriot and you can be proud of your son, he won't cause you any more sorrow. I'll try to write, but it will be difficult—soon we'll be leaving Brittany for an unknown destination. Don't worry, Mother, I'll be careful. I'm with former NCOs, hunters, and very dear friends.

As I was saying, Mother, I won't be able to see you until the country is completely liberated, which I hope will be soon. Mother, I have to ask you for a favor: *1 pair of socks and 1 shirt* from the old mended clothes. If you have the chance, please pack them in a little satchel with 1 muffler (1 of mine) and my raincoat, although I know it will be next to impossible as there's no way to communicate, and M.J. will already be carrying a lot.

Don't tell Papa about my having enlisted—he'd be worried, and I've already hurt him too much. Tell Annick to give Papa my ration cards; there's no shortage of tobacco here!

Say hello to all my friends, Madame and Monsieur Bernard Henri Lavanenay, and everyone else. Tell them that I'm in the countryside and haven't forgotten about them.

I must leave you, Mother, I'm being called for a patrol.

Courage! Vive la France!

See you very soon! Victory is ours!

Your son, Martial[35]

On the back of Martial's letter, preserved today in the archives, are written the following words: "Letter of Martial Cloarec of Quimper, who died in battle at Nivot. Original conserved by his father."

RETURNING HOME

As the battlefield moved out of the Cotentin Peninsula, hundreds of thousands of refugees began to make their way home. Often what they found was a deathscape, hardly recognizable, in which very little if anything remained. When sixteen-year-old Jacques Petit returned to Saint-Lô some weeks after the American victory there, he was overwhelmed.

> My city, Saint-Lô, no longer exists. A few weeks of madness was all it took to destroy my childhood stomping grounds. How can I get back what I've lost? How can I pick up the pieces of my past in these streets that have been reduced to dead-end paths fraught with uncertainty?[36]

Similarly, a witness identified as Yvonne did not recognize her hometown of Mortain when she returned in August. A terrible German counterattack had occurred there a few weeks before.[37] She and eight hundred other civilians had survived by holding out in the caves of a local mine for two weeks.

> We couldn't bear to look around us. It was hell. Everything had been destroyed. The dead animals on the roadside were bloated due to the early August heat. The corpses of soldiers were decomposing in the embankments and orchards. We returned to discover a pestilent odor of death hanging over the countryside. I had never seen a dead person in my life. I tried to avert my eyes, but there were so many corpses on the ground that it was impossible. While this was happening, we crossed paths with a convoy of trucks filled

with soldiers giving us the V sign and tossing us cigarettes, chewing gum, and bars of chocolate.

This was it; this surreal, spectacular combination of deliverance and death was the Liberation that we dreamed of for days on end in the depths of the mine. We reached the house with Grandmother; by some sort of miracle, it was still standing. The Americans had commandeered it for use as an emergency first-aid station. The rooms were a complete mess: the closets had been emptied, and there were mattresses stacked on the floor. An American showed us the bullet-pierced helmets of his fallen brothers in arms. It was at that moment, when we left the mine, that the full horror of the war hit home. I found myself face to face with the reality and heartbreak of it: the dead, the wounded, the amount of destruction caused by the bombs . . .[38]

Thousands of Normans experienced such a homecoming. A bomb crater marked the place where their homes once stood. If by some miracle a home remained standing, it usually lacked a roof or windows. Doors had been removed to use as trench covers. Precious belongings were smashed or gone. Both the Germans and the Allies engaged in looting.

MAKING FRIENDS

By mid-August, the Allies were victorious in Normandy. Under the command of Omar Bradley, the American First Army moved south and east out of the Cotentin, trapping thousands of Germans in the "Falaise pocket" between Falaise and Argentan. Hitler ordered his armies in Normandy to retreat. The Allies then began to move rapidly east toward Paris.

As the bombing and the bullets subsided, Americans and Normans finally got to know each other better. Friendships were forged. Key to those attachments, at least at the beginning, was American munificence. The US Army had provided the GIs with presents for Normans: cigarettes for adults and candy for children. The troops carried such treats in their pockets or distributed them from trucks. The idea was to break down barriers between the French and the Americans by offering gifts. The gesture was wildly successful. The abundance and wonder of American products made a deep impression on the Normans.

Friendship drew from additional sources that summer. The GIs missed their kids and siblings and so made Norman children their own, at least for a little while. Many of these children, themselves missing fathers, happily climbed onto laps and gave big hugs. Soldier and civilian also shared a heavy heart for what had been lost.

For both, the war was real, and they were in it together. They came together to grieve, sing, feast, dance, and even have a little fun.

LUCKIES AND HERSHEYS

The GIs liberated, yes—but perhaps more important, they brought cigarettes. "Not only have they come to render a sacred service," Paul Finance gushed about the Liberation, "but they've also offered me a pack of cigarettes!"[1] If the Americans loved Calvados, the French loved "blond" American cigarettes. For years, smokers had been almost entirely deprived of tobacco. Now the GIs offered it to them in abundance. Jacques Petit's memory of his first American is inseparable from his first Lucky Strike. On August 2, he told his journal:

> The tanks knocked down the gates without hesitation and positioned themselves in the surrounding fields. Everywhere there were flowers, bravos, and hands raised with parted fingers in the victory sign. The soldiers threw candy and little packs of three or four cigarettes. My first American smoke, a Lucky Strike! I had only tasted tobacco a few months earlier, and my father, who didn't smoke (that day I would see him make an exception for the first and last time in my life), granted me one pack of Gauloises per month from his rations. After several weeks of almost no smoking and the blandness of German cigarettes, this honey-flavored smoke was a delicacy![2]

Fifteen-year-old Jacques Nicolle was shocked to see even his mother smoking: "Our liberators made sure to give us rations and sweets, which is how I started smoking at fifteen (although I quit for good a year later). That is why I tell my students . . . , 'My smoking is ancient history.' I think I even remember seeing my mother puffing on a cigarette!"[3] Albert Desile's memories of his liberation are also inseparable from the cigarettes he and his friends received. In his diary of August 3, he wrote:

> Above the turret of each armored vehicle was a chest-up view of a helmeted soldier wearing headphones, throwing candy and cigarettes galore. We didn't venture into the jostling crowd that formed as a result, but were still able to lay our hands on a few packs. Monsieur Yver, laden with Camels and Raleighs, was on cloud nine! After having to get by with the bare minimum for quite some time, he was now smoking like a chimney![4]

Normans who were children in 1944 remember, above all, the candy. The GIs fell in love with Norman children. "I'll have to break down and admit that they were the most beautiful children I have ever seen," wrote journalist Ernie Pyle.[5] Young Normans were more than happy to return the compliment: As Charles Lemeland remembers in the pages that follow, "the Americans were nothing but demigods haloed with a kind of supernatural prestige." Key to that godly status was the secret supply of candy every GI stocked in his pockets. Generous amounts of Hershey's chocolate found their way into tiny Norman hands, courtesy of the US Army.

That was just the start. Take, for example, the case of little Lucien Lepoittevin. With his mother, he set up a sort of lemonade stand, only Norman-style—for cider. He did so on Route 25, a road heavily trafficked by the GIs. For soldiers too hurried to get out of their trucks, Lepoittevin offered window service. But for payment, he expected more than the usual.

> At first, we were surprised by their opulence and the munificence of their gifts, but the smallest ones—chocolate, cigarettes, and chewing gum—soon lost their value simply because there was an overabundance of them. That said, we were always eager for orange marmalade, fruit preserves, and other little ingenious rations with

everything combined. Yielding to our bold entreaties, the nice fellows smilingly let us strip away part of their uniforms. That was
how I was able to build up an unrivaled collection of stripes and
insignia.[6]

The GIs had a habit of being bamboozled this way. They would
do just about anything to make kids happy. Despite army rules, no
child who ventured into a mess hall with spoon in hand ever went
away hungry. The GIs would take much more food than they could
eat, then pass it on to the children. Norman kids reminded them of
beloved ones back home. One GI showed ten-year-old Marguerite
Madeleine a picture of his little girl.

Our liberators had set up their mess in the little field around the
house, which was again uninhabited. From time to time, they
would give us white bread with spread, which for us was a sumptu-
ous delicacy. Once the gherkins or jam had been eaten, our big glass
jars were filled with chewing gum. My brother and I chewed the
gum with delight, under the disapproving eyes of our parents, who,
although fearful it would upset our stomachs, didn't dare scold us.

I also remember one day when I happened to be near the military
camp and a soldier came up to me, smiling. He leaned down to my
level and held out a photo of a little girl my age—surely a daughter
or little sister that I reminded him of. I felt very self-conscious, and
he put the photo back in his card case as he walked away to catch
up with his friends. I hope that he got home safely.[7]

Chewing gum was another gift, and relatively new to France. At
first, the youngest Normans couldn't figure it out. Do you just keep
on chewing? Six-year-old Marcel Launay wondered whether his
gum would make his teeth fall out. He hardly cared, though, and
carefully parked it under his pillow every night.[8] Danièle Philippe
lived in coastal Normandy not far from the docks where American

surplus arrived. Even after the front had moved away from Normandy, Cherbourg and Le Havre remained key ports, where everything from bullets to surgical scissors to gasoline arrived every week. And of course enough fruit, meat, cheese, and chocolate to feed the liberators. Some of it inevitably got "lost" along the way.

> Military trucks passed with a deafening roar along the road behind our house. Curious as ever, Colette, Michel, and I ran to the wide-open gate at the entrance to the factory. A procession of eight big trucks drove by us, each with its lights on. The black drivers waved at us enthusiastically, their proud, white-toothed smiles gleaming on their black faces. We were so taken aback by this that we stood silent, petrified. They threw candy and tiny packages in our direction all the same.
>
> Standing on a platform on the last truck, the soldiers threw heaps of goodies. Once the convoy had left, we began to collect our unexpected booty. We didn't really know what chewing gum was or what we were supposed to do with those funny little sticks. There were also cigarettes—each packet individually sealed—that had surely been given to them just before the landing, as had the brownish-beige chocolate that tasted funny.[9]

Many Norman children recall African American soldiers in particular. The job of unloading and transporting gasoline, food, and armaments to the front became the responsibility of service troops, many of whom were black.[10] Norman children had ignorant ideas about Native American and African American soldiers. But they remember them as smiling and generous. Five-year-old Yves Boudier had this child's perspective on his liberators:

> During the Liberation, every day was like a Sunday: the church bells never stopped ringing. . . . Most of all, there were Americans. It's funny, they come from the country of the Indians and Buffalo

Bill, but they don't have red skin. No, their skin is the color of the big pieces of chocolate that my grandfather caught behind the convoy of open-topped trucks. One of them threw me up in the air. I touched him, and afterward my hand wasn't dirty. We were also given packs of clear, round candy with a hole in the middle and a funny taste that I didn't know.[11] They were good.

Those Americans, they laugh all the time and have white teeth and wear their helmets backwards. They are always eating "chouine-gomme" [chewing gum]. There were no women with the soldiers. They didn't even bring mothers with them to heal them when they became sick. They also drink coffee and hot chocolate from big, gray pitchers made of a really lightweight metal called aluminum.[12]

THE MAGIC OF FOOD

American food was a source of wonder. GI rations included such dehydrated drinks as juice, milk, and coffee. Children watched with fascination as orange, white, and brown powders were magically transformed into familiar drinks. Christiane Delpierre remembers:

Sometimes I would have breakfast with them. There was a sort of magical quality to it. Think about it, I had always seen milk coming from the teat of a cow, but they had a sort of white powder that they would pour on water. And the coffee? Brown grains! When mixed with warm milk, it would turn into coffee similar to ours. At our house, making coffee was a laborious task. We had to grind the beans in a wooden mill that I would struggle to crank as I held it between my knees, pinching my thighs.[13]

Marcel Leveel from Lison was also in awe of American rations.

First there were the thin cigarettes. I recognized certain brands such as Camel and Philip Morris, which we had before the start of the war. Then I rediscovered chewing gum, which I had tasted during a family vacation in Paris. They also had little aluminum foil packages with a powder used to make drinks. By adding water, they were able to make orange and lemon soda. And to purify water, they had tiny bottles of pills. But what surprised me the most was that they used products I thought were French, like the little packets and cans of Nescafé. We had those products before the war. I also picked up a little bar of Palmolive soap. As a child, I had never imagined that all these products that we knew fairly well were manufactured abroad! We also received canned goods marked "Pork," "Beans," and—much to my surprise—"Cheese." Canned cheese? I also found a "Cheese and Ham." Their rations also included full meals labeled "Ration K." Inside there was everything needed for a hearty snack: cookies, a canned good, chocolate, a powdered drink, and even a case of five cigarettes.[14]

Little boys were drawn to the military vehicles and equipment. Little Jacques-Alain de Sédouy, living in Vire at the time, remembers the American jeep.

Five jeeps pulled up in front of the stoop. Amid the droves of men and women warmly shaking hands with the soldiers, my father was speaking to an officer, recognizable by stripes under the flaps of his canvas jacket. The windshields of the jeeps were folded down onto the hood. Our liberators, who were seated inside chewing gum or leaning nonchalantly on the vehicles, had an air of friendly superiority about them. Despite the fervor of the encounter, there was a distance between them and us, a gulf of power, wealth, and victory.

I approached the jeeps, wide-eyed. Who could have thought up such a vehicle? Their square shape gave them the look of big junebugs. The interior was a world in and of itself. Rustic yet comfortable, there was a large, round steering wheel and two canvas seats up front, with a bench seat in back, behind which the metal-framed top folded down. Here and there were packs, ammunition boxes, and, for the jeeps with machine guns, several metal cases filled with strips of cartridges. It had everything one needed to be self-sufficient: on the back, there was a big spare tire and a jerry can for gasoline tied down with canvas straps; a wooden-handled shovel and pickaxe were mounted on the sides. In the place of doors, there were two large notches in the body of the vehicle that almost beckoned you to jump in—it was a microcosm of the efficiency and openness of American society.[15]

Twelve-year-old Charles Lemeland was also fascinated with American military gear and equipment. Lacking knowledge of American sports, he wondered why the GIs threw balls at each other while wearing big gloves.

Friendly, good-humored, and good-looking, they were quite popular, especially with women. Best of all, they did not look or act like fanatical, professional soldiers. As if they did not take the war quite seriously or, at least, not all the time. They had a great talent for enjoying themselves whenever they could. We were fascinated by their demeanor, their gestures. In a word, they were "cool." The way they got into their cars and drove was classy, with a touch of wildness. We could not figure out why they threw balls at each other endlessly, or why they would want to use those ridiculously big gloves. Strange soldiers. Right in the middle of a campaign, they had time to play. They were definitely a different breed of cats.

The baggy shape of the American uniform was another surprise. We were used to the tight-fitting garments of the Wehrmacht. Black hobnailed boots were now replaced by a soft, civilized walking item often covered by those strange canvas leggings. Armies have their own particular smell. The German soldier combined those of leather, soap, and tea. Not bad, but no match for the precious and novel perfumery the American army had to offer: peppermint, doughnut, and American tobacco.

What impressed us most was the US war materiel. First, the unimaginable quantities: thousands of trucks and cars. German military vehicles always had a wickedly purposeful look. Compared to the mean-looking Panther tank, the American Sherman did seem rather laid back, like an unaggressive crustacean. American trucks and cars were like civilian trucks and cars that had been painted to assume a warlike stance. That cocky, lovable little jeep was an immediate hit. Made for war but maybe for fun also! We were dying to get a ride in one. My sister, who was in a boarding school and had not been heard of since the end of May, was brought back to us by an officer of the US Army Civilian Branch. She made a splendid appearance in a jeep. She was the lucky one![16]

The myth of America as a land of abundance was not new to the French, but it gained new force in the war years. The United States became virtually synonymous with material wealth. The occupation had been a time of scarcity and hardship, as the Germans had drained France of its coal, oil, and every imaginable foodstuff. Women queued for hours every day for a meager piece of meat or a small piece of bread. Then came the Americans with their huge supplies of rations, coffee, chocolate, cigarettes, and toiletries. Here is Jacques-Alain de Sédouy's youthful impression:

America was a land of plenty. For me, the little European who had known only the hardships of war, there were untold treasures concealed under the lids of the two trunks in the back of the jeeps. Like the White Man offering cheap trinkets to an African tribe, the soldiers were generous in their gifts of chocolate, cigarettes, candy, and chewing gum. One such treat was a round, orange fruit with a thick peel. A soldier gave me one, and I ran over to my sister.

"Look! What is this?"

"It's an orange," she answered. "It's really good, you'll see. I'll teach you how to eat it. We'll share it, and I'll give you half my chocolate."

We went and sat behind a bush, and I watched in amazement as she skillfully cut off a long twist of peel, revealing the thin white membrane that covers the flesh of the fruit. Then she split it into quarters, squirting juice between her fingers in the process. With the eagerness of a boy taking his first Communion, I bit into the fleshy, sweet fruit from California or Florida.[17]

For Normans, an orange was an extravagant luxury. Citrus fruit had all but disappeared from Europe since the beginning of the war. Gérard Rabiller also remembers a precious orange given by a black soldier driving supplies to the front.

A cool wind was blowing in from the nearby sea on that November morning. I was standing on the sidewalk near my mother, who was chatting away, as do all the housewives of the world. To pass the time, I was reminiscing about the endless procession of white-starred GMCs [General Motors Corporation]. On one side were all the empty trucks rolling down avenue de Paris toward the port; on the other were all the resupplied trucks, brimming with equipment as they set out for the far-away front.

At that moment, the convoy traveling uphill was stopped right in front of me. I could see the driver of one of the trucks, a strapping fellow whose helmet nearly touched the roof of the cabin. He was looking back at me, wide-eyed, his big smile revealing a set of sparkling white teeth. Still smiling, he waved hello to me. I think he even said something that I couldn't hear because of the engine noise. Then he started motioning to me! His raspy voice was muffled, but I could hear bits and pieces. I wasn't quite sure what this ebony-skinned stranger wanted, with his big smile and waving hands. He seemed to grow impatient with my passivity, as if he wanted me to participate in the exchange.

All of a sudden, he leaned forward and disappeared from my sight, reappearing after a few seconds. In his hand was a big yellow ball that he held out to me with an almost shy smile. He clearly wanted to give it to me as a gift. Instinctively, I clung to my mother's skirt. She had been watching the whole scene, and said, "Take it, take it! That's an orange! Thank you, sir! Thank you, sir!" Comforted by my mother's reassurances, I went up to the truck and received my first orange. It was wonderful! It was so big that I had to hold it in both hands! It shone like the sun through the clouds on an autumn day. I was hypnotized by the ball and its unfamiliar smell, which was both sour and sweet. My mistrustful demeanor had the GI in stitches to the point where he was slapping his knees with joy, as if he had just played a good joke on someone.

My mother urged me on, "Say thank you to the gentleman, say thank you!" I at last opened my mouth and yelled, "Thank you!" My black friend must have heard what I'd said, because a big burst of laughter filled the cabin. Then he calmed down and just smiled. At the time, I didn't understand why his attitude had changed, why he was suddenly sad. Thinking about it later, I was sure that it wasn't me that had caused it, because his happiness wasn't at all feigned. Maybe giving me that gift made him think of another little boy who was waiting for him back in his country.

And then, after one last glance, one last smile, and one last wave, my big black soldier started his truck back up and went back on his way with the others. I stood there sheepishly, still holding the orange in both hands. I wondered what a real orange was like. I say "real," because I had already seen a fake one in a celluloid fruit basket that decorated the buffet in the dining room. It had a bunch of grapes, a fuzzy peach, and a yellow banana with black dots. I still remember the smell of that artificial celluloid fruit—nothing like my real orange![18]

CHAPTER SIX

"THE WONDERFUL WORLD OF LAUGHTER, PLAY, AND PERMISSIVENESS"

When the GIs stayed in an area for a few days or so, they formed attachments with local children. Refugeed at a relative's house in the western Cotentin, Charles Lemeland became good friends with some GIs who camped nearby. Again, his memories are shaped by the gifts he received, but also by the pinup photos so popular with the American soldiers.

One morning late in July, when we had settled down at a relative's house, we woke up to find the woods around us, the Forest of St. Sauveur-Le-Vicomte, alive with bivouacking soldiers of the US Third Army. A good number of these soldiers were New Englanders, and some spoke a French dialect that we had little difficulty understanding. We children had always remained a safe distance from the German soldiers. Not that we were afraid of them, but rather because they represented another form of adult authority which did not appear to really understand us, or at least had limited patience with us. We did not trust them, just as we did not trust any teacher and many adults.

With the American soldiers, it was the wonderful world of laughter, play, and permissiveness: candy galore, the thrill of getting inside tanks and other fascinating machinery and touching all those levers and pedals, posing for pictures, looking at pictures of relatives, of girlfriends usually in bathing suits and appearing to us like movie stars! We wondered if it was sinful to even look at them. Would we have to mention that in confession?

The soldiers stayed about a week, I think. And it was one of the most exciting weeks of my life. My brother and I visited *les Américains* from morning to night. We came home with unimaginable gifts: a pair of army boots that hopefully, in a year or two, would fit me; loads of things to eat, all as well packaged as perfume bottles; and, greatest of all, a small tent. The Eldorado had come to us. The

172

Americans were nothing but demigods haloed with a kind of super-natural prestige.

One evening, two demigods came for dinner, Roland Chareat of Nashun [Nashua], New Hampshire, and Victor Bouvier of Marl-boro, Massachusetts. I don't know how my uncle had succeeded in inviting them. He was a very warm and convincing man. My father was surprised that soldiers about to go into battle would accept such an invitation. My aunt was a great cook and made a very fine meal. The women in the house thought that the two Americans were charming and most handsome. I was in awe.[19]

So many Norman children were fatherless during the war. Roughly two million Frenchmen were prisoners, laborers, or de-portees in Germany. Thousands of others were serving in the French army or fighting for the Resistance. As a result, the GIs filled an emotional need for these children, as demonstrated by the story of six-year-old Francine Leblond.

The war really broke out in 1939, but my story took place in 1944. I was six years at the time, sick with polio and hence forced to rest in a carriage.[20] From there I witnessed the Germans and the days of massacres, which took place under my eyes. My father was taken prisoner [by the Germans], so I lived with my mother and my grandparents. Then we had to take to the roads, where we risked our lives, ironically in order to save them. From Marigny we went to Ouville, which then became our refuge, where we were taken in by two old women.[21] Then the Americans arrived. One of them found the place peaceful and decided to rest in the barn of the house. This would have been fine if another soldier had not also chosen the barn as a shelter. And not just any soldier, mind you, but a German! Despite their differences, however, they became close friends, and played the harmonica together every day. One day, the American noticed my presence and took me in his arms. I was thrilled, because my father was gone, and I considered this stranger as my "adoptive" father. He had his binoculars with him at all times, and he showed me the planes as they flew overhead. If he heard the least worrisome noise, he would part quickly for the barn, but he always made sure to leave me in a sheltered place. He called me Francisca because, he told me, it reminded him of his own country. Perhaps he lived in San Francisco. I believe his name was William. He was about twenty years old, a very big man, with blue eyes and blond curly hair, pale skin, and a round face. Then the rest of his compatriots arrived. According to my grandfather, he was obliged to kill his friend in order not to appear to be a traitor in front of the other soldiers. When he left, I was absolutely inconsolable.[22]

Leblond was not the only child bereft by the departure of a GI. Christiane Delpierre also felt abandoned after discovering the pleasures of being a little girl in a GI camp. When the Americans came to stay a few days near her refugee family, she quickly made friends.

Engines roaring, they set up camp one fine morning in an extensive pasture on our farm/animal sanctuary. Their "depot" was buzzing with activity. The specialists bustled about, preparing the new equipment for combat and repairing damaged equipment. They had put up huge tents—I would have really liked to have stepped inside. I couldn't think of anything more enjoyable than sleeping in a tent. I was emboldened to approach the depot and look in through the hedge that had been lined with barbed wire. . . .

My first "official" visit was with my father. Hand in hand, we took a tour of the facilities. There was no danger of not getting along with the Americans, because that would have required us to be able to communicate. But they didn't speak our language, and we didn't speak theirs. They nonetheless welcomed us kindly and invited us to tour the grounds. I almost added "down to the very last detail," but frankly, I've no clue. They probably let us see what they wanted us to see, and nothing more. Plus, I had a limited attention span for tanks and artillery. I was well aware of the havoc they could wreak. I had a hard time believing my father's assurances that they would do us no harm. I preferred to keep my distance, and was more curious to see the tents where the soldiers slept and ate. But our guide had no idea that we could be interested in anything other than weapons and equipment—an expression of his country's power—and he didn't lead us to the areas I had hoped.

In any case, I was a hit (it seems that soldiers always welcome girls, even the young ones), and went home with pockets bulging with chocolate, candy, and chewing gum. My father also received his fair share of gifts, mostly Camel cigarettes and canned goods. I made a habit of visiting our neighbors, and would do so unless my parents forbade it. There was always someone there to welcome me. One day, a GI asked me what my name was.

"Christiane."

"Oh, yeah! Christine."

"No, Christiane."

"OK, Christine."

To tell the truth, I didn't mind the name "Christine." I found it pretty.

And so it was that "Christine" became my passport into the depot with the GIs. "Hello, Christine!" they would shout from near and far. It seemed as if I'd become the regiment's mascot. I'd have my picture taken on the knees of one soldier and in the arms of another; perched on top of a tank, wearing a helmet, or with a garrison cap over one ear, at the wheel of a jeep. I was living the glorious life of a star. It's a shame not to have any photos to go along with my memories. . . .

I would play soccer and basketball with them. They would hold me up so that I could score a basket. Our games were often interrupted by German aircraft overhead. At the least sign of trouble, I would find myself in a hole with three or four guys, who would cover me as protection. Once the danger had passed, we would keep on playing, with cannon fire in the background.

The daytime heat was stifling. In the evening, if the area was calm, we would get some fresh air in the courtyard. A few soldiers would come and join us. They would open their wallets and take out photos.

"Mother . . . children," they would explain as they showed them.

They didn't speak French, of course, but we were able to communicate using gestures, the universal language. . . .

I wasn't all that surprised to be awakened by the noise of purring engines, clicking chains, and orders being shouted. But the racket continued, and my usual tactic of hiding my head under a pillow was of no use. I soon realized that it was coming from outside. I jumped out of bed and went to the gate of the depot—that is to say, where the depot had been. There was nothing left. The tents were gone and the holes had been covered up, leaving only big bald patches. The only thing missing was the grass, but that would grow back in time. Meanwhile, all the vehicles had lined up on the road and began their procession away from the farm in a most orderly fashion. There were command cars, jeeps, and trucks; armored vehicles, such as tanks, ATVs [all-terrain vehicles], and half-tracks; and the artillery, which was transported on other vehicles or towed.

They all waved to me—the men in the jeeps and trucks, as well as those in the tanks and artillery. I bawled my eyes out like never before for my sister, who no longer lived with us. Or rather for the fact that on top of all my friends leaving, she was gone, too. I was all alone, a girl abandoned by everyone around her.[23]

Danièle Philippe's friendship with a GI began with a misunderstanding. Because of her blond, braided hair, an American captain mistook her for a German girl. "No German!" she corrected him. "Norman girl blue eyes, too!" Apologetic, the captain, whose name was Marco Previti, invited Danièle and her sister (with her parents' permission, of course) to tour the American Red Cross hospital. Philippe described the tour in her diary of June 15:

During our afternoon class, Captain Previti came to pick us up. The fact that he had kept his promise made a big impression on us—and on our parents! They immediately took a liking to the American officer, and gave us permission to go with him.

"I'm going to show your three children around our tent village, and I'll bring them back myself, safe and sound. Captain's honor!"

Riding in a jeep for the first time, taking in the air with delight, we were exhilarated by the fresh breeze of freedom and adventure that had blown our hair and our minds in a state of disarray. We suddenly took a knock and were shaken about rather roughly. The captain slowed down and proceeded with caution over the strange perforated-metal sheet that covered the entire width of the road. We were soon at the pasture where the Red Cross was located. They had pitched five tents, two of which were quite large. Captain Previti showed us his tent—one of the smallest ones—and we each took a turn swiveling and reclining in his wonderful dentist seat. It was a hundred times better than the one in which we had spent anxious moments at the dentist's office in Caen. Everything else in the tent was astonishingly modern, comfortable and spotless. . . .

On the way back, we spotted an airplane taking off behind a row of trees in a pasture that we were fairly sure belonged to us. Previti drove us over, and we were right: the long, narrow pasture was part of the dairy farm. The Americans in the field gave Previti a hearty greeting worthy of his own friendly nature, which seemed typical of military men. We were introduced. The jokes began to fly, and so much was said in so little time that we barely understood a quarter of it! The Air Force officer seemed completely relaxed with his men. I wondered if all American officers were so friendly and at ease with their subordinates.

"It's a little tight," the officer said, "but I'm sure Bob will make it. Don't be afraid!"

Worried all the same, we looked on as the Piper made a landing attempt, gliding down toward us in a masterly slip. It skimmed the ground but didn't touch down; then, with an impressive roar, it pulled up just in time to clear the line of trees.

"He's not going to make it," Michel said under his breath. "The pasture isn't long enough."

But a few minutes later, the pilot made a picture-perfect landing and taxied in our direction across the makeshift airfield. "Bob" cut the engine, pressed a few buttons, and finally opened the cockpit. Beaming with pride, he made the two-fingered "V for victory" sign. Everyone congratulated one another, and during the ensuing conversation with our friend Previti, Bob promised to take us in his airplane once the front was a little farther away.

This offer and all our other experiences with the Americans were the main topic of conversation at dinner. We were so talkative that Papa couldn't help but smile.

"Haven't I always told you that the Americans are no ordinary folks?"[24]

Accustomed to the rigidly hierarchical German army, Normans were surprised by the easy relations that seemed to prevail between American officers and their men. Normans interpreted this fact as a sign of a true democracy.

HOME AWAY FROM HOME

Adults made friends, too. A few days after Philippe's outing with Captain Previti, her parents invited over another American for dinner, an intelligence officer from California. In her diary of June 17, Philippe talked about the visit, at once sad and fun.

Mom came back with a tray full of glasses. Her spontaneous sense of hospitality was on full display that evening. There were all the makings of an interesting night, and in the end it was an unforgettable one.

We all gathered in the living room. The first thing that caught the colonel's eye was the piano. He asked Mom if he could play, and immediately launched into a fairly difficult Rachmaninoff piece, which he performed with astonishing gusto. We were greatly impressed—and very surprised at the unexpected turn that the evening had taken. The colonel informed us that the Russian had passed away the previous year in Beverly Hills:

"I was very moved because I love Russian music and live in Santa Barbara, California."

The colonel suggested that Mother sit down at the piano herself. She politely declined:

"You're such a virtuoso that I don't feel up to it." She began to look in the chest of drawers for sheet music, some old melodies in English that she had known since the First World War. Gleaming with pride, she brought the colonel a packet of yellowed, timeworn sheets.

"Sorry!" she said. "I played these songs so often that all these songbooks are rather worse for wear."

"Splendid!" he exclaimed, surprised and visibly delighted. "You have got 'My Little Grey Home in the West.' I love this song."

It was no accident that Mother had put this romantic song from the Far West at the top of the pile. I knew that we were in luck! Over time, it had become one of our family's favorite tunes. We had grown up with it. When we were children, babies even—well before we were able to understand the lyrics—Mother had sung it to us as a lullaby. Our mother always loved to sing, and we would listen, swiftly calmed and enthralled. We found this particular song particularly moving, because we were drawn into the setting it depicted, this wonderful world of pioneers. Were we not in the "Far West" of our own continent?

First the colonel played the melody, then turned to us and said cheerfully:

"Now it's time to sing all together. Let's go!"

His cordiality was contagious, and in any case, we wanted nothing more than to please him. We all huddled around the piano. The colonel had a pleasant voice that was rich and warm.

"There are hands that will welcome me in. There are lips I am longing to kiss. There are two eyes that shine, just because they are mine. And a thousand things others may miss. In my little grey home in the West."

The colonel was surely thinking about California as he sang this verse. Were there palm trees where he lived? The song was finished, but the melody was still fresh in the air. Singing together had brought us closer together. We were all touched by the moment. Did the feeling of togetherness surprise us? Something much more serious must have taken place for an Intelligence Service officer to become so overcome with emotion.

"I beg your pardon!" he said. "A tragic event befell me recently, and it's always in the back of my mind. My boy died June 6 at Omaha. He was part of the first wave. Joe was twenty-one years old and full of pluck. I was thinking of my wife, who has to endure this all alone at home." At that point, we were the ones who were filled with emotion. What incredible self-control he had, this American colonel! Papa silently went over and shook his hand. We remained where we were.

Later, together we drank the last bottle of champagne we had in the cellar. Everyone had some, even us children. It wasn't a party, but in a certain way it was. Never had we imagined that mourning, elation, fear, and hope could mingle as they did that evening.[25]

As we have already seen, Normans frequently opened their doors to homesick Americans, putting their best food on the table. The young Jacques-Alain de Sédouy remembers one occasion when his father invited an entire regiment of officers for dinner. Preparations took days, and no expense was spared.

Via an American officer of Swiss extraction who spoke perfect French, my father invited the entire US regiment that had liberated us to lunch. Three days was barely enough to prepare all the rooms on the ground floor, refurnish them, sweep and wax the wood floors, dust the crystal chandeliers, and clean the silver, which had been hidden in the cellar with the set of Sèvres porcelain flower bouquet plates that we used for special occasions.

The big day arrived. I have never seen such a superb sight. Decorating the center of the table was a biscuit sculpture depicting, amid cherubim and wreaths, an almost fully unclothed lady breastfeeding a baby while a similarly undressed man gazed at her pensively. I've been told it is an allegory representing conjugal bliss, a wedding gift to my great-grandparents that brought them little good fortune (they spent their lives bickering). Little bouquets of orange and red dahlias on either side of the table added a stroke of color, accompanied by a hint of dark ruby in the form of the wine, which was decanted in crystal carafes. High bronze and copper chandeliers featuring classical goddesses added a finishing touch to the elegant, balanced table.

I wasn't allowed to sit at the table, but I did have permission to stay in the dining room and help with the service if I could. Three young girls from neighboring farms were tasked with lending a hand. They had been breaking their backs since the morning, while mother Morel tended to the stove. Around noon, from the kitchen I heard a few jeeps pull up in front of the doorstep. About twenty officers, led by a corpulent colonel, got out and followed my father into the house. Following a glass of champagne introduced by the peaceful detonation of several flying corks—my father had undoubtedly used a method at which he excelled: slicing the tops off the bottles with a saber—the officers sat down around the table. There was no particular protocol. My mother, perched on her cork high heels, in a green polka-dot dress with a discreet low-cut neckline, had made a special effort to do justice to Paris's reputation for fashionable elegance. She was sitting across from her husband and to the left of the heavyset colonel. The other guests had chosen their seats as they wished. The conversation started off slowly, but picked up as the meal went on. The white wine served with the hors-d'oeuvres and the red wine with the leg of lamb surely had a hand in that.

Sédouy's father then decided it was time to teach the regiment the *trou normand*, or "Norman hole." In a matter of minutes, he brought the great conquering army to the floor.

At the midway point, my father quieted everyone and explained that it was time for the traditional *trou normand*. I can only guess how the interpreter translated the name for this little glass of Calvados that, on my father's signal, everyone drank down in one gulp. I watched closely as the scene unfolded and saw faces pucker and blush. Several attempted to muffle a hoarse hiccup, and there was even a young lieutenant who disappeared under the table for a moment. Everyone pushed their chairs back, discreetly fanned themselves, and tried to catch their breath.

After this shock treatment, the second half of the lunch—chicken in cream sauce, mixed greens, cheeses, and an omelets flambé with cognac—went off without a hitch. A heartfelt jollity began to take hold. An officer stood up and retrieved the family's old gramophone, from which protruded a large funnel-shaped horn, and placed a record on the turntable. It was a one-step by Jelly Roll Morton and the Red Hot Peppers. He asked my mother for a dance. Soon, my sisters were also led onto the dance floor, then the three young servants. For mother Morel, who had been invited out from the kitchen to receive praise for her cooking, the introduction to jazz was a bit more difficult. She made a valiant effort, however, as those around her clapped the rhythm to help. This was met with whistles from our guests, showing their enthusiasm for these Europeans with their strange culinary traditions who were more than willing to take in some American culture.

After a cup of coffee, washed down with Calvados and cognac, a few officers felt like getting some fresh air. In the entryway, they discovered a bag of golf clubs that belonged to my uncle. They lined up in the front yard—which had been mowed that same morning—and laid out about fifty little white balls taken from an old shoebox that was sitting next to the bag. They began to take turns hitting drives. I looked on, amazed at the way they swung their bodies with the left arm straight as an arrow, all while keeping their eye on the ball. Their arm would swoop down, we would hear a thwack, their body would finish its slightly curved rotation— like a bow bending back into shape—their hands would follow through above their head, and the ball would fly beyond the big cedar some two hundred meters away.

One of the officers had extraordinary power and precision. He could hit the ball within a few meters of his target while chomping on a cigar the size of a chair leg. His face dripping with sweat, he would stop between each shot and stifle a burp before returning to the tee, with his buddies cheering him on.[26]

THE CATHEDRALS

The wounds of Normandy did not heal quickly. The winter of 1944–45 was grueling and cold, even though the front was now hundreds of miles away. With so many factories in ruins, jobs were few and far between. Food was still rationed, still scarce, and still tasteless, despite Allied efforts to feed a starving Europe. At Christmastime, the Caen newspaper *La Liberté de Normandie* declared it "the saddest Christmas we have ever known. Because we still live in a world in flames, in a murdered France, in a ravaged region. No more houses, no more roofs over our head, and grief everywhere around us."[1] The year 1944 had brought freedom but also ruin and death.

Still another set of challenges would arrive with the new year. Like everyone else, Normans celebrated the long-awaited victory over the Nazis in May. But the spring and summer of 1945 were far from euphoric. Slowly but surely, relations between the Americans and the Normans had soured. As the US troops made the nation its garrison, they created a black market in army surplus. Sometime during the late summer of 1944, the GIs had realized that their Lucky cigarettes and Hershey chocolate were valuable commodities. Soon they were hawking them for brandy and sex, taking advantage of French scarcity. Increasingly for the Normans, cigarettes became a symbol not of liberation but of American exploitation and corruption.

But the trouble really began in the spring of 1945. With the war over, the GIs made their way back west to Norman ports and ultimately a boat home. Even those who had survived came back to Normandy as changed men. Traumatized by the awfulness of war, grieving losses both big and small, they took to the bottle to relieve their pain. They drank, they whored, they drove their jeeps too fast. In cities like Le Havre, overrun with GIs by midsummer, Normans frequently found themselves in the wrong place at the wrong time. Almost every day, someone was injured by a recklessly driven jeep, shot by errant bullets, or assaulted by drunk men with guns.

Worse still were the prostitutes. Civilians in places like Mourmelon, Reims, and again, Le Havre, could not take a walk in the park or visit their mother's grave without witnessing the spectacle of a GI having sex with a prostitute in broad daylight and out in the open. American soldiers also accosted "respectable" Frenchwomen, even in the presence of their husbands and boyfriends. One mayor called his town "a theater of military debauchery."[2]

French mayors complained loudly. It did little good. The US Army refused to create regulated brothels for its soldiers. To do so, the high brass explained, would be tantamount to letting journalists and the American public know that the boys were doing more than fighting in France. Hence GI promiscuity remained a rude reality for French civilians in order to protect American wives and sweethearts back home. In addition, US commanders in garrison towns refused to take responsibility for the thousands of prostitutes now suffering from venereal diseases. In all these ways, the US military flaunted their disregard for French sexual and social norms. Civilians returned the favor with anger and contempt. The Americans had overstayed their visit. It was time for them all to go home.[3]

The Normans also felt a seething resentment toward the Allies for the physical destruction they had endured. Given the difficult finances of the French state, reconstruction was slow in coming. Among the most tragic casualties of the battle had been the cathedrals, many dating to medieval times. In the mid-twentieth century, these churches remained at the heart of their community, symbolizing its lifeblood. Shortly after the war, Father Georges Cadel mourned his church in Coutances.

During these dark times, the people of Coutances displayed a touching love for their cathedral. At an aid station the night of the first bombing, a wounded man who had been pulled from the ruins of the prison was greatly comforted to hear the bells toll to mark the hour. "At least the cathedral hasn't taken heavy damage," he said. "The clock is still ringing." During the subsequent bombings, many refugees watched from the surrounding hills as the planes swooped down over Coutances in the moonlight. They were constantly worried that it would be hit. The refugees were especially watchful on the night of June 13–14, when the outline of the cathedral appeared in stark contrast to the sky. Unlike during the Fêtes du Millénaire celebration in 1933, when floodlights illuminated the cathedral, this time it was the sinister glow of a fire devouring nearby houses.

From then on, the exiled population was constantly concerned about its fate, as much as—and sometimes more than—that of their own possessions. In homes where several families were staying, when someone did a bit of salvaging in town, the first question they would be asked was, "And the cathedral?" . . .

We felt that the cathedral really was the heart of the city. As long as it was standing, Coutances would survive; houses would be rebuilt around it, like a cherry forming around a stone. If it fell, the feeling was that Coutances could be destroyed forever or have to be rebuilt elsewhere.[4]

FIGURE 3. The cathedral in present-day Coutances, France. Photograph copyright Amy Ralston.

The Coutances cathedral became a sign of hope. It was the core around which new life could grow. To destroy the church was to destroy the city itself. Its reconstruction meant the city's rebirth.

In 1945, still another priest was grieving his beloved church, this time in Guidel, Brittany. For him, however, it was the greatness of Allied sacrifice that engendered hope.

The church was built from 1838 to 1841, then expanded from 1860 to 1881 in a classical style featuring semicircular arches and a fifty-six-meter steeple with Doric, Ionic, and Corinthian columns. Once a sight to behold, it has been reduced to rubble. The roof, which was hit several times and partially caved in, needs to be rebuilt completely. The gaping holes in the walls do little to conceal the sorrowful sight. The steeple was hit in the shelling and collapsed on February 3. Underneath the resulting heap of stones are the remnants of our beautiful set of four bells, weighing a total of 4,340 kilograms.

What is more, the beautiful molding from the gallery is buried, our elegant pulpit demolished, the artistic stained glass windows shattered, and our massive organ scarred. The paneling in the choir also suffered heavy damage, as did the marble altar and most of the furniture in the church. The majority of chapels in the surrounding countryside were hit during the shelling, shattering all their windows, at a minimum. Not one room in the rectory was salvageable. The entire building has to be rebuilt, along with so many other homes in a fairly large radius around the bell tower, which for months served as a target for the Americans.

All this destruction will certainly make for a lengthy and difficult economic recovery. Considering the extent of our current hardships, the country will not return to normal for a very long time. But Guidel will stand strong, for its cemetery is the final resting place for 137 American and British Allied soldiers who gave their lives for a sacred cause: freedom. We placed signs of our profound respect and heartfelt gratitude around their earthly remains, and consider the brave, selfless sacrifice of these generous soldiers as a clear assurance that Guidel will rise up from the ashes.[5]

Normans made sense of the ruins by viewing them within a larger pattern of Allied sacrifice. Despite their dismay over bad GI behavior, they were grateful for their liberation. From the hell of battle, they had learned to prize the gifts they were given. Sixteen-year-old Jacques Petit, who returned to his native Saint-Lô only to find it completely destroyed, wrote to his diary on August 31:

What will stay with me from this experience, this series of terrifying situations, preposterous turns of events, trying mishaps, and thrilling moments that defy all logic? My youthful frivolity and inexperi-

ence came up against hardships for which nothing could have prepared me. I discovered forgotten worlds deep in the countryside
and met their inhabitants. I saw the Germans, some of whom only
a few months my elder, suffer a crushing defeat. American wealth,
poise, organization, and efficiency swept through with unexpected
force. Before me was hope, enthusiasm, the future . . . life. I cherish
it even more so, because it could have been taken away.[6]

ACKNOWLEDGMENTS

The travel, research, and translation work required for this project were generously funded by the University of Wisconsin–Madison Graduate School. I am indebted to Professor Susan Cook and the Graduate School Research Committee for having made *D-Day through French Eyes* possible. A special thanks to Professor Robert Asen, who so ably presented my case to the committee on more than one occasion. In addition, a Senior Fellowship at the Institute for Research in the Humanities has given me invaluable time away from teaching. My thanks to the IRH and Professor Susan S. Friedman for this support.

Many documents excerpted here were placed in my hands by two extraordinary archivists: Alain Talon at Les Archives départementales et du patrimoine de la Manche, and Stéphane Simonnet, Directeur Scientifique at Le Mémorial de Caen. I thank them both for their generosity, expertise, and warm welcome. Ethan Footlik did the lion's share of the translations, always with efficiency, elegance, and grace. I am so grateful for his exceptional gifts as a translator. Thanks as well to Kelly Jakes, who provided superb research help. As always, the A-team at the University of Chicago Press—Susan Bielstein, Anthony Burton, Sandra Hazel, and Levi Stahl—immeasurably improved *D-Day through French Eyes*, all with wit and good humor. I appreciate their efforts to work on a tight schedule so that the book could be published at a timely moment. With their meticulous readings of the manuscript, the two anonymous readers for the press saved me from several errors. Many thanks to them for taking the time to give me such helpful and incisive criticism.

My greatest debt by far is to my partner, Susan Zaeske, who has made this project possible in ways too numerous to mention. I am so very lucky to have her in my life. With profound gratitude and love, I dedicate this volume to her.

NOTES

INTRODUCTION

1 This collection varies in both tone and content from my previous book on the Normandy campaign, *What Soldiers Do: Sex and the American GI in World War II France* (Chicago: University of Chicago Press, 2013). That shift arises, in part, from my focus on the first weeks of the invasion, when relations between GIs and civilians were not yet troubled by looting and sexual violence. Also different here is my purpose: to present an overview of the Norman experience rather than a critical, in-depth study of Franco-American relations.

2 H. R. Kedward, *Occupied France: Collaboration and Resistance, 1940–1944* (Oxford: Blackwell, 1985), 75.

3 See Jean Quellien and Bernard Garnier, *Les victimes civiles du Calvados dans la Bataille de Normandie: 1er mars 1944–31 décembre 1945* (Caen: Éditions-Diffusion du Lys, 1995), 13–20; William I. Hitchcock, *The Bitter Road to Freedom: A New History of the Liberation of Europe* (New York: Free Press, 2008), 27–28. Total casualties for France by the end of World War II were 217,600 military deaths and an estimated 350,000 civilian deaths.

4 See Rick Atkinson, *The Guns at Last Light: The War in Western Europe, 1944–1945* (New York: Henry Holt, 2013), 55.

CHAPTER ONE

1 The paratroopers were given clickers, small devices that made cricket-like sounds. They were to signal to each other using these sound-makers, probably the source of the "strange crackling sound."

2 The plan for the 82nd Airborne Division was to land on both sides of the River Merderet and from there take the town of Sainte-Mère-Église.

3 Mémorial de Caen, TE 277, Marcelle Hamel-Hateau, "Des mémoires d'une petite maîtresse d'école de Normandie, souvenirs du débarquement de juin 1944." The account is dated "circa 1944."

4 The Nord is a department of France that covers the northernmost tip of the country along the western border of Belgium. Falaise and Caen are both cities directly to the north of Ferté-Macé.

5 Bernard Gourbin, *Une jeunesse occupée: De l'Orne au Bessin; 1940–1944* (Le Coudray-Macouard: Cheminements, 2004), 85–87.

6 This is not an original diary. Instead, it was written as a memoir in diary form by its author in the 1980s.

7 A large bay to the southeast of Cherbourg and Sainte-Mère-Église that cuts into the Cotentin Peninsula from the east.

8 A nickname given to the Cotentin Peninsula, which means "the almost-island of the Manche." The Manche is the department or regional name given to that peninsula, which is surrounded by water on three sides.

9 Cécile Armagnac, *Ambulancières en Normandie, Cherbourg-Caen, 1944* (Barbary: Éditions du Moulin vieux, 1994), 47–49.

10 Val de Saire is the name given to a region in the northeast corner of the Cotentin Peninsula.

11 Mémorial de Caen, TE 207, Suzanne Bigeon (née Arnault), "Journal tenu pendant les jours précédant la Libération de Cherbourg: Le Débarquement. Les Allemands. Les Américains." Bigeon wrote the original diary in 1944. In 1979–80, it was revised and edited by Colette Arnault.

12 Michel Boivin, Gérard Bourdin, and Jean Quellien, *Villes normandes sous les bombes (juin 1944)* (Caen: Presses Universitaires de Caen, 1994), 10.

13 The Flying Fortress was a very large Allied bomber, the Boeing B-17.

14 Michel Béchet, *L'attente: "Overlord" vécu à cent kilomètres du front* (Montsûrs: Éditions Résiac, 1994), 21–22.

15 Antoine Anne, *J'aurais aimé vous conter une autre histoire* (Saint-Georges d'Elle: A. Anne, 1999), 59–60.

16 Le Rachinet was a sort of refuge, fifteen hundred meters from the house and two kilometers from the train station (a constant target for bombing).

17 A group of French people taking refuge together in nearby Moon-sur-Elle.

18 Marcel Leveel, *Rails et haies: La double bataille de l'Elle et de Lison* (Marigny: Éditions Eurocibles, 2004), 47–48. Leveel based this memoir on a journal that he had written at the time.

19 Moreau's account is written in the form of a diary, but it was completed as a memoir in 1989.

20 Mémorial de Caen, TE 284, Yvette Moreau, "Le Liseron froissé." Moreau wrote this memoir in 1989.

21 Charles de la Morandière, quoted in *La Bataille de Normandie: Récits et témoins*, ed. René Herval (Paris: Éditions de "Notre temps," 1947), 1:189–90.

22 Mémorial de Caen, TE 610, Jacqueline Sabine, "Souvenirs de débarquement et de la Libération du 6 juin au 25 août 1944."

23 Despite Roger's use of the present tense in some parts of his account, the following is a memoir recorded by Roger in 1984, forty years after the landings.

24 Organisation civile et militaire, a resistance movement during the war. See Guillaume Piketty, "Organisation civile et militaire," François Marcot (dir.), *Dictionnaire historique de la Résistance* (Paris: Éditions Robert Laffont, 2006).

25 Dufour is the alias given to a man named Junger who was making arrests for the Gestapo in Saint-Lô. It is not clear from the account whether Junger was German or French. At this point in the war, several of Roger's friends had been arrested by Junger.

26 Jean Roger's memory is faulty here. Neither Franklin D. Roosevelt nor Charles de Gaulle spoke on the radio until the evening of D-Day. General Eisenhower gave a speech to the troops on the eve of the invasion.

27 German military headquarters in Saint-Lô.

28 Jean Roger, quoted in Boivin, Bourdin, and Quellien, *Villes normandes sous les bombes*, 187–96.

29 Diary of J. de Saint-Jorre, in Herval, *Bataille de Normandie*, 1:85–87.

30 Mémorial de Caen, TE 641, Témoignage de Madame Hardouin.

31 Danièle Philippe, *J'avais quinze ans . . . en juin 44, en Normandie* (Paris: Éditions France-Empire, 1994), 96–101. According to Atkinson, *Guns at Last Light*, 56, three thousand tons of bombs fell just inland from the Norman shore on the night of June 5–6, for a raid that lasted an hour and a half.

32 Anthony Beevor, *D-Day: The Battle for Normandy* (London: Penguin Books, 2010), 74.

33 Pierre Ferrary, quoted in Herval, *Bataille de Normandie*, 1:37–39.

CHAPTER TWO

1 Max Hastings, *Overlord: D-Day and the Battle for Normandy* (London: Michael Joseph, 1984), 74.

2 Atkinson, *Guns at Last Light*, 48.

3 Jeannette Pentecôte, quoted in *Chroniques du Jour J*, by Gilles Bré (Paris: Éditions Christian, 2006), 58–59.

4 Archives départmentales de la Manche, Saint-Lô (hereafter ADM), 1366 W, Comité vérité historique, *Liberté 44, la Manche témoigne: De l'occupation à la libération; Les Manchois se souviennent* (hereafter 1366 W), Témoignage de Madame Odette Eudes, 333.

5 Both Turqueville and the hamlet of Loutres are a few kilometers east of Sainte-Mère-Église.

6 Maurice Mauger, quoted in Bré, *Chroniques du Jour J*, 64.

7 Gliders were small planes carrying equipment, such as jeeps, that was too heavy to be brought in by parachute.

8 Mémorial de Caen, TE 587, Jean Flamand, "4–6 juin 1944." Flamand misremembered the time of his encounter with the parachutist, who, as a member of the 82nd Airborne, landed a few hours after midnight. He wrote this memoir in 1948.

9 Mémorial de Caen, TE 587, Flamand, "4–6 juin 1944." In fact, jeeps came in by glider rather than parachute.

10 L'Abbaye is on the western perimeter of Rémilly-sur-Lozon.

11 The Organisation civile et militaire was a movement of the Resistance. See note 24 in chapter 1 above.

12 This castle is just north of the town of Rémilly-sur-Lozon.

13 Mémorial de Caen, FN 62, Georgette Leduc, "Mon mari fusillé."

14 Marcel Jourdain, *Petites surprises de printemps* (Le Chaufour: Éditions Anovi, 2004), 104–7.

15 Amfreville was north and east of Prétot, just to the west of Sainte-Mère-Église. These *paras* had been dropped several kilometers too far south; they were most likely members of the 82nd Airborne Division.

16 Michel Birette, quoted in Bré, *Chroniques du Jour J*, 181–82.

17 Edouard Marie, *Souvenirs d'un marin pêcheur de Chausey* (Granville: Éditions Formats, 1995), 73–75.

18 ADM, 1366 W, Témoignage de Christian Letourneur, 732.

19 Fernand Levoy, quoted in Association historique et culturelle de Montebourg et son Canton, *Montebourg se souvient, 6 juin–19 juin 1944* (Condé-sur-Noireau: Éditions Charles Corlet, 1994), 53.

20 Ibid., 54–55.

21 The Kommandantur was the German military headquarters in Montebourg.

22 Eugene Legoupil, quoted in Herval, *Bataille de Normandie*, 1:107–8.

23 Hastings, *Overlord*, 211.

24 Hérouvillette is to the north and east of Caen and only a few kilometers from the coast.

25 Mémorial de Caen, TE 598, Témoignage de Irène Othon-Meillat.

26 Mémorial de Caen, TE 341, "M. Henri Manach, gendarme à Caumont-l'Eventé, évoque ses activités avec ses collègues lors de la Libération," 1993. Most likely, these soldiers were British rather than American, as it was the British who had dropped or landed in the region of Caen.

27 Mémorial de Caen, TE 277, Hamel-Hateau, "Extrait des mémoires."

28 Ibid.

29 Denise Boursier-Lereculey, quoted in *Paroles de braves: D'Omaha la sanglante à Saint-Lô, capitale des Ruines, 7 juin–18 juillet 1944*, by Claude Paris (Condé-sur-Noireau: Éditions Charles Corlet, 2007), 32.

30 Mémorial de Caen, TE 701, S. Pezerin, "Souvenirs de la Libération, 6 Juin 1944."

31 These Mongolians were probably prisoners of war from the Soviet Union client state established as the People's Republic of Mongolia in 1924. The Nazis used imprisoned Soviet soldiers as both soldiers and workers, particularly toward the end of the war, when they suffered manpower shortages.

32 Mémorial de Caen, TE 701, Pezerin, "Souvenirs."

33 In his account of the events at Graignes, G. H. Bennett also describes a French-woman bursting into the church to warn the soldiers, but names her as Madame Bazir. See his *Destination Normandy: Three American Regiments on D-Day* (Westport, CT: Praeger Security International, 2007), 121.

34 Michel Folliot, quoted in Paris, *Paroles de braves*, 37–38. Sergeant Boussard is not included in Bennett's historical account of Graignes, *Destination Normandy*. Major Johnson was killed in the course of the battle on June 11.

35 Mémorial de Caen, TE 701, Pezerin, "Souvenirs."

36 ADM, 1366 W, Témoignage d'Odile Delacotte, 233–35.

CHAPTER THREE

1 Andy Rooney, *My War* (New York: Random House, 1995), 166, 161.

2 Les Perruques is a street in Maisy southwest of the center of the town.

3   Madame Destors, quoted in *Cahiers de mémoire: Vivre et survivre pendant la Bataille de Normandie*, ed. Béatrice Poulle (Caen: Conseil général du Calvados, 1994), 18–19.

4   Fernand Broekx, quoted in Herval, *Bataille de Normandie*, 1:31–35.

5   Eddy Florentin, *Quand les alliés bombardaient la France* (Paris: Librairie Académique Perrin, 1997), 335, 408.

6   Boivin, Bourdin, and Quellien, *Villes normandes sous les bombes*, 19.

7   Philippe, *J'avais quinze ans*, 104.

8   Mémorial de Caen, TE 610, Jacqueline Sabine, "Souvenirs de débarquement et de la Libération du 6 juin au 25 aout 1944." Raymond was Sabine's fiancé.

9   Jacques Perret, *Caen, 6 juin 1944, une famille dans le débarquement* (Paris: Éditions Tirésias, 1994), 53.

10 This hospital was most likely run by the Catholic Church. In this case, an adjacent cloister would have housed the nuns, who served as nurses.

11 Yvonne Mannevy, quoted in Boivin, Bourdin, and Quellien, *Villes normandes sous les bombes*, 33–39.

12 Hitchcock, *Bitter Road*, 44.

13 Paris, *Paroles de braves*, 146–48.

14 Ibid.

15 Mémorial de Caen, TE 277, Hamel-Hateau, "Des mémoires."

16 Janine Guérin, quoted in Boivin, Bourdin, and Quellien, *Villes normandes sous les bombes*, 147–51.

17 Dada is the French equivalent of Parcheesi.

18 Mémorial de Caen, TE 207, Bigeon, "Journal tenu."

19 ADM, 1366 W, Témoignage de Madame Colette L'hermitte, "La Bataille de Carentan."

20 ADM, 1366 W, Témoignage de Désiré Pottier.

CHAPTER FOUR

1   The landing force also included members of the Polish and Free French armies.

2   According to Atkinson, *Guns at Last Light*, 74, Vierville had fallen by ten o'clock that morning except for a few snipers.

3   Mémorial de Caen, FN, Trevières, Témoignage de Victorine Houyvet.

4   Mémorial de Caen, FN, Trevières, Témoignage de Marguerite Gidon.

5   Mémorial de Caen, FN, Trevières, Témoignage de Jacques Bailleul.

6   "Tommies" was a nickname for British soldiers.

7   Mémorial de Caen, TE 448, Jean Roy, "Et les souvenirs meurent aussi . . . Vauville 1939–1945."

8   ADM, 1366 W, Témoignage de Jean-Jacques Vautier.

9   Hastings, *Overlord*, 245.

10 Atkinson, *Guns at Last Light*, 113.

11 Gastebled most likely ran the local café in town.

12 ADM, 1366 W, Christiane Denis, "La Libération de Fleury."

13 Gourbin, *Une jeunesse occupée*, 110–13.

14 The Signals Corps soldier was probably using wire cutters, not pliers.

15 Could this have been a Camel cigarette, with a drawing of a pyramid and a camel on the box?

16 Leveel, *Rails et haies*, 90–91.

17 Mémorial de Caen, TE 105, Témoignage d'Yvette Travert.

18 Jacques Petit, *Au coeur de la Bataille de Normandie: Souvenirs d'un adolescent, de Saint-Lô à Avranches, été 1944* (Louviers: Ysec, DL, 2004), 85–87. The author was sixteen when his home in Saint-Lô was invaded and destroyed. He wrote the memoir years later based on a diary he had kept at the time.

19 The Cross of Lorraine was a double-barred cross that became Charles de Gaulle's symbol of the resistance movement Free French Forces during the war.

20 Ferrary, quoted in Herval, *Bataille de Normandie*, 1:46.

21 ADM, 1366 W, René Docloue, "Souvenirs d'une famille, famille réfugiée des bombardements de Saint-Lo."

22 Abbé H. Dufour, in Abbé H. Dufour and Lucien Voisin, *La Guerre chez nous: Le Lorey, 1940–1944* (Marigny: Eurocibles, 2004), 42. Abbé Dufour was the parish priest of Le Lorey from 1940 to 1953.

23 Ibid., 43–44.

24 ADM, 1366 W, Témoignage de Claude Bourdon.

25 Mémorial de Caen, TE 105, Témoignage d'Yvette Travert.

26 Albert Desile, *Des sombres années de l'occupation aux chemins de l'été 1944* (Coutances: Éditions OCEP, 1983), 135, 137. Desile was originally from Saint-Lô but was in Vendel, farther south, when his liberation occurred. His memoir is based on a diary he had kept during the summer of 1944.

27 Mémorial de Caen, TE 448, Roy, "Et les souvenirs meurent aussi."

28 Perhaps this bar was a "chocolate D ration," developed in 1937. Besides chocolate, it contained oat flour and skim milk flour. It was believed to give the GIs high energy. See http://en.wikipedia.org/wiki/United_States_military_chocolate.

29 Mémorial de Caen, FN, Trevières, Témoignage de Janine Chambrin.

30 Abbé Georges Cadel, quoted in Herval, *Bataille de Normandie*, 1:183.

31 The meaning of "shock troops" here is probably "frontline soldiers."

32 Mémorial de Caen, FN, Trevières, Témoignage de Marie Jeanne Leneveu.

33 Mémorial de Caen, TE 208, Madame Mahier, "Le Débarquement."

CHAPTER FIVE

1 Monsieur Darondel, quoted in Herval, *Bataille de Normandie*, 1:28–30.

2 ADM, 1366 W, Témoignage de Madame Fenand dit soeur Christine Yvonne, 342.

3 Mémorial de Caen, FN 62, Normandie hors Calvados, Rémilly-sur-Lozon, Témoignage d'Albert Lehodey.

4 The shelter was on the rue du Clos Vautier in Rémilly.

5 Témoignage d'Albert Lehodey.

6 Ibid.

7 Gustave Marie, quoted in Paris, *Paroles de braves*, 154–55.

8 These threats appear to be real, as many people, including the elderly, who refused to evacuate and stayed behind were found dead after the Liberation.

9 Normandy is a well-known horse-breeding region.

10 "Two Germans dead."

11 Mémorial de Caen, TE 587, Flamand, "4–6 juin 1944."

12 ADM, 1366 W, MT, Témoignage d'Odette Eudes, 333.

13 Juliette Brault, quoted in Bré, *Chroniques du Jour J*, 144–45.

14 ADM, 1366 W, MT, Anonymous, "Le Débarquement," 1017.

15 Daniel Fossey, "Une famille rurale dans la guerre (sous le mitraillage à Carantilly, en exode jusqu'à Beslon) juin-juillet-août 1944," *Journal de la Manche* 36, no. 142 (April 1994): 72–73.

16 ADM, 1366 W, MT, Témoignage de Madame Fenand dit soeur Christine Yvonne, 342.

17 Gustave Marie, quoted in Paris, *Paroles de braves*, 154–55.

18 Mémorial de Caen, FN, Rémilly-sur-Lozon, Témoignage d'Arsène Quinette, "Le Cri des enfants."

19 ADM, 1366 W, Témoignage de Christian Letourneur, 732.

20 Mémorial de Caen, FN 62, Normandie hors Calvados, Rémilly-sur-Lozon, Témoignage de Désiré Pottier, "Les Paras Prisonniers."

21 Mémorial de Caen, TE 587, Flamand, "4–6 juin 1944."

22 The French manufacturers of Cadum soap used a baby to advertise their product. The pudgy, blond "Cadum baby" became a familiar advertising feature.

23 Leveel, *Rails et haies*, 167.

24 ADM, 1366 W, Témoignage de Désiré Pottier, 436–38.

25 Maurice Allix, quoted in Association historique et culturelle de Montebourg et son canton, *Montebourg se souvient*, 149–51.

26 Ibid.

27 ADM, 1366 W, Journal de Michel Braley, 105. Braley's family lived in Saint-Lô, but was exiled farther south to Condé-sur-Noireau during the war.

28 ADM, 1366 W, Témoignage de Raymond Avignon, 28–30.

29 ADM, 1366 W, Témoignage de Georgette Leduc, 433.

30 Beevor, *D-Day*, 381, 384.

31 The Gendarmerie is a French military unit in charge of maintaining order, especially in rural areas.

32 Archives départementales du Finistère, Fonds Roger Bourrières, 202 J 9, Libération du Finistère après le 6 juin 1944: Rapports, récits, témoignages. Région Nord, "Rapport de M. Abily, Jean cultivateur."

33 Beevor, *D-Day*, 384. Twenty-five civilians were shot in St. Pol-de-Léon on August 4, and forty-two men, women, and children were shot in Gouesnou on August 7.

34 The *maquis* initially referred to a geographical landscape in Corsica, made of small shrubs and brush and very difficult to penetrate. During World War II, it designated a place, generally far from the cities, where members of the Resistance could gather, hide, and conduct guerilla warfare.

35 Archives départementales du Finistère, 208 J 189, "Combat de la libération: Arrivée des Américains en Bretagne."

36 Petit, *Au coeur de la Bataille de Normandie*, 116.

37 The German attack at Mortain took place on August 7, 1944.

38 Yvonne, quoted in Philippe Bertin, *Histoires extraordinaires du jour le plus long* (Rennes: Éditions Ouest-France, 2004), 81–82.

CHAPTER SIX

1 Paul Finance, *Trois ans de ma vie, 1942 à 1945* (Riquewihr: La Petite Imprimerie, 1993), 117.
2 Petit, *Au coeur de la Bataille de Normandie*, 85–86.
3 ADM, 1366 W, Jacques Nicolle, "J'avais quinze ans."
4 Desile, *Des sombres années*, 135, 137.
5 Ernie Pyle, *Brave Men* (New York: H. Holt, 1944), 285.
6 Lucien Lepoittevin, *Mémoires de guerres (1692–1993)* (Cherbourg: Isoéte, 1994), 104.
7 Mémorial de Caen, TE 695, Marguerite Madeleine, "Mes souvenirs du débarquement de Normandie."
8 Launay, *6 ans en 1944*, 18, 37.
9 Philippe, *J'avais quinze ans*, 144.
10 With very few exceptions, African American soldiers were forbidden from combat positions during World War II.
11 Could these be the candy Lifesavers?
12 ADM, 1366 W, Témoignage de Yves Boudier, 100–102.
13 Christiane Delpierre, *Une enfance normande* (Angers: Cheminements, 1999), 148–51.
14 Leveel, *Rails et baies*, 104–5.
15 Jacques-Alain de Sédouy, *Une enfance bien-pensante sous l'occupation, 1940–1945* (Paris: Librairie Académique Perrin, 1998), 152–53.
16 Charles Lemeland, quoted in Hilary Kaiser, *Veteran Recall: Americans in France Remember the War* (Paris: Author, 1994), 89–90.
17 Sédouy, *Une enfance bien-pensante sous l'occupation*, 152–54.
18 Mémorial de Caen, TE 586, Gérard Rabiller, "Méli-Mélo: Une enfance normande."
19 Lemeland, quoted in Kaiser, *Veteran Recall*, 89–91.
20 There was no vaccine for polio until the mid-1950s.
21 Ouville is a small village in the lower Cotentin Peninsula, southwest of Coutances.
22 ADM, 1366 W, Témoignage de Madame Francine Leblond, 650–51.
23 Delpierre, *Une enfance normande*, 149–51.
24 Philippe, *J'avais quinze ans*, 149–51.
25 Ibid., 164–66.
26 Sédouy, *Une enfance bien-pensante*, 158–63.

CONCLUSION

1 *Liberté de Normandie*, 23 December 1944.
2 Archives départementales de la Marne, 161 W 323, Incidents franco-américains, rapports, 1944–46, report dated June 26, 1945.
3 For a fuller explanation of these developments in French-American relations, see Roberts, *What Soldiers Do*.
4 Father Georges Cadel, quoted in Herval, *Bataille de Normandie*, 1:176–77.
5 Archives départementales du Morbihan, Fonds du Comité d'Histoire de la Deuxième Guerre Mondiale, Témoignages, 41 J 40, La Poche de Lorient, Témoignage par Abbé Picard, May 1945. Guidel is just west of Lorient on the southern peninsula of Brittany.
6 Petit, *Au coeur de la Bataille de Normandie*, 122–23.

BIBLIOGRAPHY

ARCHIVES

Mémorial de Caen, Caen
    Series TE and FN
Archives départementales de la Marne, Reims
    161 W 323, Incidents franco-américains, rapports, 1944–46
Archives départementales et du patrimoine de la Manche, Saint-Lô
    1366 W, Comité vérité historique, *Liberté 44, la Manche témoigne: De l'occupation
    à la libération; Les Manchois se souviennent*
Archives départementales, Morbihan, Vannes
    Fonds du comité d'histoire de la deuxième guerre mondiale, Témoignages,
    41 J 40
Archives départementales du Finistère, Quimper
    Fonds Roger Bourrières

PUBLISHED WORKS

Anne, Antoine. *J'aurais aimé vous conter une autre histoire.* Saint-Georges d'Elle:
    A. Anne, 1999.
Armagnac, Cécile. *Ambulancières en Normandie, Cherbourg-Caen, 1944.* Barbary:
    Éditions du Moulin vieux, 1994.
Association historique et culturelle de Montebourg et son Canton. *Montebourg
    se souvient, 6 juin—19 juin 1944.* Condé-sur-Noireau: Éditions Charles Corlet,
    1994.
Atkinson, Rick. *The Guns at Last Light: The War in Western Europe, 1944–1945.* New
    York: Henry Holt, 2013.
Béchet, Michel. *L'attente: "Overlord" vécu à cent kilomètres du front.* Montsûrs: Édi-
    tions Résiac, 1994.

Beevor, Anthony. *D-Day: The Battle for Normandy*. London: Penguin Books, 2010.

Bennett, G. H. *Destination Normandy: Three American Regiments on D-Day*. Westport, CT: Praeger Security International, 2007.

Bertin, Philippe. *Histoires extraordinaires du jour le plus long*. Rennes: Éditions Ouest-France, 2004.

Boivin, Michel, Gérard Bourdin, and Jean Quellien. *Villes normandes sous les bombes (juin 1944)*. Caen: Presses Universitaires de Caen, 1994.

Bré, Gilles. *Chroniques du Jour J*. Paris: Éditions Christian, 2006.

Delpierre, Christiane. *Une enfance normande*. Angers: Cheminements, 1999.

Desile, Albert. *Des sombres années de l'occupation aux chemins de l'été 1944*. Coutances: Éditions OCEP, 1983.

Dufour, Abbé H., and Lucien Voisin. *La Guerre chez nous: Le Lorey, 1940–1944*. Marigny: Eurocibles, 2004.

Finance, Paul. *Trois ans de ma vie, 1942 à 1945*. Riquewihr: La Petite Imprimerie, 1993.

Florentin, Eddy. *Quand les alliés bombardaient la France*. Paris: Librairie Académique Perrin, 1997.

Fossey, Daniel. "Une famille rurale dans la guerre (sous le mitraillage à Carantilly, en exode jusqu'à Beslon) juin-juillet-aout 1944." *Revue de la Manche* 36, no. 142 (April 1994): 72–73.

Gourbin, Bernard. *Une jeunesse occupée: De l'Orne au Bessin; 1940–1944*. Le Coudray-Macouard: Cheminements, 2004.

Hastings, Max. *Overlord: D-Day and the Battle for Normandy*. London: Michael Joseph, 1984.

Herval, René, ed. *La Bataille de Normandie: Récits et témoins*. Vol. 1. Paris: Éditions de "Notre temps," 1947.

Hitchcock, William I. *The Bitter Road to Freedom: A New History of the Liberation of Europe*. New York: Free Press, 2008.

Jourdain, Marcel. *Petites surprises de printemps*. Le Chaufour: Éditions Anovi, 2004.

Kaiser, Hilary. *Veteran Recall: Americans in France Remember the War*. Paris: Author, 1994.

Kedward, H. R. *Occupied France: Collaboration and Resistance, 1940–1944*. Oxford: Blackwell, 1985.

Lepoittevin, Lucien. *Mémoires de guerres (1692–1993)*. Cherbourg: Isoéte, 1994.

Leveel, Marcel. *Rails et baies: La double bataille de l'Elle et de Lison*. Marigny: Éditions Eurocibles, 2004.

Marie, Edouard. *Souvenirs d'un marin pêcheur de Chausey*. Granville: Éditions Formats, 1995.

Paris, Claude. *Paroles de braves: D'Omaha la Sanglante à Saint-Lô, capitale des Ruines, 7 juin–18 juillet 1944*. Condé-sur-Noireau: Éditions Charles Corlet, 2007.

Perret, Jacques. *Caen, 6 juin 1944, une famille dans le débarquement*. Paris: Éditions Tirésias, 1994.

Petit, Jacques. *Au coeur de la Bataille de Normandie: Souvenirs d'un adolescent, de Saint-Lô à Avranches, été 1944*. Louviers: Ysec, DL, 2004.

Philippe, Danièle. *J'avais quinze ans . . . en juin 44, en Normandie*. Paris: Éditions France-Empire, 1994.

Piketty, Guillaume. "Organisation civile et militaire." In *Dictionnaire historique de la Résistance*, edited by François Marcot. Paris: Éditions Robert Laffont, 2006.

Poulle, Béatrice, ed. *Cahiers de mémoire: Vivre et survivre pendant la Bataille de Normandie*. Caen: Conseil général du Calvados, 1994.

Pyle, Ernie. *Brave Men*. New York: H. Holt, 1944.

Quellien, Jean, and Bernard Garnier. *Les victimes civiles du Calvados dans la Bataille de Normandie: 1er mars 1944–31 décembre 1945*. Caen: Éditions-Diffusion du Lys, 1995.

Rooney, Andy. *My War*. New York: Random House, 1995.

Sédouy, Jacques-Alain de. *Une enfance bien-pensante sous l'occupation, 1940–1945*. Paris: Librairie Académique Perrin, 1998.

INDEX